D1039753

ON BEING CATHOLIC

The material herein first appeared in slightly different form in the column, "From My Viewpoint" which appears on a weekly basis in the *Catholic New York*. Gratitude is expressed to the *Catholic New York* for their permission and assistance in making this material available for this book.

ON BEING
CATHOLIC

✠ John Cardinal O'Connor
Archbishop of New York

ALBA·HOUSE   NEW·YORK
SOCIETY OF ST. PAUL, 2187 VICTORY BLVD., STATEN ISLAND, NEW YORK 10314

Library of Congress Cataloging-in-Publication Data

O'Connor, John, 1920-
    On being Catholic / John Cardinal O'Connor.
          p.   cm.
      ISBN 0-8189-0718-5
        1. Youth — Religious life. 2. Catholic Church — Doctrines — Juvenile
    literature. 3. Catholic Church — Membership — Juvenile literature.
    4. O'Connor, John, 1920-   . I. Title.
    BX2355.037   1994
    282 — dc20   94-30653
                                                      CIP

Produced and designed in the United States of America by the
Fathers and Brothers of the Society of St. Paul,
2187 Victory Boulevard, Staten Island, New York 10314,
as part of their communications apostolate.

ISBN: 0-8189-0718-5

© Copyright 1994 by the Society of St. Paul

Printing Information:

Current Printing - first digit	1	2	3	4	5	6	7	8	9	10

Year of Current Printing - first year shown

1994	1995	1996	1997	1998	1999

Table of Contents

Growing Up Catholic

Mary and the Saints

Life Issues: Right to Life,
Euthanasia, Care of the Handicapped, etc.

Racism, Anti-Semitism, Social Problems, AIDS

Priesthood and Religious Life

The Year — Religious and Secular

On Being Catholic

From time to time reflections appear in print under such general titles as "growing up Catholic." I find some of these helpful, some confusing. Invariably, those that I find helpful come from individuals who are living their faith today precisely because of their roots. Those that I find confusing come from individuals who seem to write of their childhood and youth as Catholics only to criticize everything that they were taught, and by the criticism to justify their rejection of the Faith in adulthood. I feel sorry for them.

Perhaps I'm simply lucky. What was taught to me in my childhood and youth was so sound that I have never had to doubt its validity. Moreover, I was especially fortunate to see the Faith practiced everyday in my own family, and to experience a mother and father who lived it as naturally as they breathed the air around them. Consequently, I have been able to apply the faith of my childhood and my youth to the problems of my adulthood, including situations I face every day as Archbishop of New York

There is nothing startling or particularly remarkable in the reflections found in this little book. When I write each week a column for *Catholic New York* from which the reflections here have been excerpted, I simply think out loud those thoughts that were part and parcel of my childhood and youth and continue today to shape my daily activities and my responses to the world as I see it, that is, the world from my viewpoint.

John Cardinal O'Connor
August 1994

Growing Up Catholic

"Tomorrow Is a Day Uncertain"

My father had the liveliest sense of death of anyone I have ever known. For the more than 50 years I knew him, he never planned seriously for more than a day ahead, and then only with the very specific provision that he be alive, a possibility he never took for granted, and indeed rather doubted.

Management consultants would have viewed my father's attitude as a sure sign of organizational dysfunction that must inevitably have led him and the family onto relief rolls (welfare of the day). They couldn't be expected to understand that irresponsibility had nothing to do with it. On the contrary, every night I would see him lay out the beloved tools of his craft and arrange them meticulously for the next day's work. When he came home at the end of the day, nothing on earth could have kept him from cleaning those tools as though they were diamonds and putting them once again in order for the day ahead. No, it wasn't irresponsibility, or laziness, or inability to organize that precluded planning *seriously* for anything in the future; it was that he considered such planning to be very presumptuous!

Since the days of King David ("there is but a step between me and death"), no one was ever more conscious than my father that he might very well die tonight, or an hour from now. "Tomorrow is a day uncertain, and how do you know if you shall have a tomorrow?" That's out of Thomas á Kempis' *The Imitation of Christ*, but if my father had been a bishop, it would have been the motto on his coat-of-arms.

As a result of this cheerful uncertainty, my father would never issue an unconditional commitment to the future. Any commitment would begin: "If the Lord spares me." He did have variations, such as, "God willing" and "If I'm alive" (sometimes tendered, "If I'm around"). There was nothing morbid about this. It was a straightforward belief that "The Lord giveth and the Lord taketh away . . . Blessed be the name of the Lord" — and that was that.

The whole business permeated our entire family. We grew up quite uncertain about whether we would. One of us would be 16 years old tomorrow, if the Lord spared him. Another would pass algebra, God willing. It all seemed quite supernaturally natural. Rather than generate insecurity, it kept life on an even keel. Nothing could be devastatingly upsetting for very long. Job could have been the patron saint of the household, with his "My years are numbered now, and I am on a journey from which I shall not return."

Of course, my father could get a bit excessive about it all, like when my mother would be after him to get a new suit, or at least a new tie. At 50, he would resist, telling us he wouldn't be around long enough to wear it. He was telling us the same thing when he died — at 86!

As I reflect on the half century or more of our association, I ask myself what my own attitude toward life would be today if it weren't for his attitude toward death. Pope John XXIII was said to have told his associates as he was about to die that his bags were packed. That's the way it seemed every day with my father, and I suspect it's why, among other things, I have a healthy respect for frequent confession! Again, my father would have agreed thoroughly with Thomas á Kempis. "You should so order yourself in every act and thought, as if today you were about to die. If you had a good conscience, you would not greatly fear death. It were better to avoid sins, than to fly death. If today you are not prepared, how will you be so tomorrow? Tomorrow is a day uncertain, and how do you know if you shall have a tomorrow?"

I'm sure it is my father's attitude toward the ever possible proximity of death that keeps me from getting puffed up about living on Madison Avenue, with all that such implies. Swanky as it is, it's only a wayside inn on the pilgrimage.

My father died enviably. All of us were around the bedside praying quietly when he slipped into a coma, where he spent a day or two, I suspect, in telling God quite calmly that he had been around a lot longer than he had expected to be, never did buy that new suit, and felt that, God willing, it was time. God was willing.

A High Price on Loyalty

My father was a great baseball fan who could talk fondly of Rogers Hornsby and Ty Cobb and Christy Matthewson and the Big Train, Walter Johnson. But he became really euphoric only when he got on to the subject of Babe Ruth, which was every time he talked baseball, which was very often. My father would never accept the notion that Roger Maris, for example, could conceivably have broken the Babe's home run record. His was not merely the standard argument about a longer season. My father was too shrewd for that. It was the ball — the "lively" ball. For my father, it was absolutely, categorically unfair to compare *anybody* with Ruth, and that included DiMaggio and Mantle, along with Maris, because they didn't have to get up there and hit the old "dead" ball over the fence as he did (and clearly a much shorter fence, incidentally, he would argue).

At any rate, the Babe died. My father could accept that as what life is all about. What he couldn't accept, then and until the day he himself died, was that the Yankees played ball the day Ruth was buried. The Yankees played ball! The Yankees whose stadium was "the house that Ruth built." He had been mad at the Yankees before, like when he realized they sold hot dogs at ball games on Friday, but this was too much. There was no arguing with him, such as: "Dad, did you ever think maybe they played out of respect for the Babe — as a kind of tribute?" My father could give withering looks even when he was happy. None ever compared to the one I got when I pulled that one.

At any rate, and here's the point of the story, he swore off baseball totally and definitely. Wouldn't go to a game, wouldn't read the sports page or listen to the radio (no television set at the time). He stuck to it for — how long? Maybe five years? Then I insisted on getting him a television set and he couldn't resist. He even turned my mother into a fan, although she would occasionally talk about the center fielder being on the 10-yard line, or the shortstop going off tackle. Indeed, before *she* died, in turn, she could argue with anybody who talked about Roger Maris that he never broke the Babe's record. That's loyalty!

It may seem to be a radically different subject to talk about, but I suspect that what we learned about loyalty in our house says a lot about why I feel the way I do about the Church and the pope. I know that honest criticism can be a high form of loyalty, and must always be welcome. I have to wonder, however, if some of the criticisms I read about these days concerning the Church and the pope are really honest, and are motivated by loyalty. Indeed, some of the criticism seems so extraordinary to me that I find myself wondering if such critics are talking about the same Church and the same pope I know, the Church described so beautifully by Karl Adam in *The Spirit of Catholicism*:

> God permits so much weakness and wretchedness in the earthly Church just because He is good. One may even venture the paradox that the mystical Christ has taken so much weakness for Himself for our sakes and for our welfare. For how might we, who are 'prone to evil from our youth,' who are constantly stumbling, constantly struggling, and never spotless, not even in our fairest virtue — how might we gladly adhere to a Church, which displayed holiness not as a chaste hope, but as a radiant achievement? Her very beauty would be a stumbling block to us. Her glory would accuse and condemn us. How would we dare to call her, the rich and glorious, our mother, the mother of poor and wretched mortals? No, we need a redemptress mother, one who, however celestial she be in the deepest re-cesses of her being, never turns coldly away from her children, when their soiled fingers touch her, and when folly and wickedness rend her marriage robe. We need a poor mother, for we ourselves are poor.
>
> Therefore we love our Church in spite of, nay just because of, her poor outward appearance. The Catho-

lic affirms the Church just as it is. For in its actual form the Church is to him the revelation of the divine Holiness, Justice and Goodness. The Catholic does not desire some ideal Church, a Church of the philosopher or the poet. Though his mother be travel-stained with long journeying, though her countenance be furrowed with care and trouble — yet, she is his mother. In her heart burns the ancient love. Out of her eyes shines the ancient faith. From her hands flow ever the ancient blessings. What would heaven be without God? What would the earth be without this Church? I believe in One Holy Catholic and Apostolic Church.

A Baby Sister Beats a Cowboy

My sister would have no way of remembering, but it seems only yesterday for me. My own birthday preceded hers by 25 days and a number of years. My birthday had been a devastating disappointment. Having pleaded for a pony for Christmas and been denied such by a father who couldn't understand how a pony could graze in a concrete city block of row houses, or sleep in the top bunk of my bedroom, I had changed my sights for my birthday. A cowboy suit would do. The 15th of January came and went. No cowboy suit. There could no longer be any question. As soon as I could save up 15 or 20 cents, I would have no choice but to run away from home.

By the 10th of February I had only a nickel, and prospects were dim as I trudged home from school, wondering where I could turn both parents in for a new set. My father was outside the house, all smiles, waiting for me. "I have a surprise for you," he said. My heart leapt: "You got me a cowboy suit?" He turned without answering, and I followed him into the house, upstairs to the second-floor front bedroom, his and my mother's. My mother was in bed and a lady in white stood at the bedside. "I have a present for you," my mother said with a big smile, "a baby girl." I turned to the white lady with the white shoes and the white cap, and asked her hopefully if the baby was hers. I didn't know why she laughed when she said the baby was my mother's.

I was as confused as I was disappointed. Where had the baby come from? How in the world could the department store where I had seen the cowboy suit of my dreams deliver a baby, instead? What kind of parents had I come by, who would refuse me both a pony and a cowboy suit, and try to pawn off on me this baby girl? I felt the nickel in my pocket, and wondered how soon I could come up with another 10 or 15 cents.

That was eight nieces and nephews ago, but my sister's birthday never comes without my asking myself what my life would have been like had I been given a cowboy suit, or even a pony, instead of a baby sister. She was the fifth in the family. One, a brother, had died. That left three to marry, and marry they did, with more nieces and nephews, grandnieces and grandnephews than anybody in the family can count.

One hears and reads much of "family values" these days, as we are plagued with moral and social evils that make Nero's Rome look like a Sunday school picnic. Public policy shapers and decision makers in a variety of categories wring hands, make plans, design programs, develop educational systems. School authorities tell us their services must broaden to include babysitting for teenage student parents, contraceptive programs to prevent teenage student pregnancies, after-school programs for children of working parents, evening programs, weekend programs.

In the meanwhile, we are all encouraged to bemoan the erosion in "family values," as long as we don't try to teach them in our public schools, or legislate them into our public policies, or finance them in our public budgets — or, above all, of course, apply them in our child care agencies.

Where in the world are we going? What do we really mean in our glib speeches about "family values"?

It would take another essay to present my own viewpoint on

such questions, and they have little to do with my sister's birthday. What has a lot to do with my sister's birthday, however, is that I had a great gift of parents who knew how and when to say no to us kids, and who taught us that over the long haul a baby sister beats a cowboy suit hands down.

I'm blessed beyond many by a fine relationship with my older brother and sister and their multitudinous children and grandchildren. As with many families, however, circumstances intertwined that baby sister's life and mine more intimately than with the others I likewise love. She married my best friend. Their eight children became, in many ways, mine. And now that as happy a marriage as the world has ever known has ended in a heart attack, my sister is widowed, and her children, all grown, look to their uncle as another link with the father they loved.

No priest could be more fortunate. After the first five-minute shock of being confronted with a baby sister, instead of a cowboy suit — much less, a pony — I decided I'd invest my nickel in her future, instead of running away from home. Every Feb. 10 I count the return on my investment. This year makes me the richest man in the world.

Summer Sun . . . and Memories

A bright summer day inevitably brings a flood of memories.

It was on just such a summer day that my mother and father might well have taken us to Atlantic City, a trolley car, a ferry boat and a steam train away, a steam train with open windows, if one preferred cinders in the eyes to suffocation. How they did it will always be beyond me. Since at my age and state in life I never intend to do it myself, I can afford to simply shake my head in wonder, without having to learn their technique, but I will always wonder.

We were four kids (one of the original five had died), of varying degrees of obstreperousness proportioned to our ages, going on a safari that would have tempted Stanley and Livingstone to stay home.

Nor was it merely negotiating the public transportation that mattered, although, given the reality of one-train-a-day-each-way, with ferry timed accordingly, such negotiation was vital. But what did you do when you got there? Why, you headed for the beach, of course, which meant you had to change into a bathing suit (they were never called anything else) in a cold, damp "bath house" under the cold, damp boardwalk, before you ran out to the hot, scalding sand. So in we would go, including my mother, up to her ankles. It took a lot of faith if the water was cold, more if it was full of seaweed, far more if filled with jellyfish, alternately called stingers or man-o-wars.

Effective sun lotion was unknown in those days, so we could be certain my father's lips would puff and bleed for days after the trip, and that all of us would be dutifully showered with corn-flour when we got home, which I suspect made our sunburn a lot worse by blocking the air from our skin! In effect, we could all expect a week of misery following a day in the sun, sand and sea.

How did they do it? Who knows but other parents? *Why* did they do it? That I don't have to guess about for a split second. They really, truly, honest-to-goodness loved us. About that there can't be a shadow of a doubt. That's what parents who loved their kids did. They took them on trips they must have dreaded taking them on, even if they could afford to do it only one day in a whole summer. They took them on a trip in the summer for the same reason they worked themselves to the bone and worried them-selves sick for the rest of the year, to put food in their kids' mouths and shoes on their feet. They did it for the same reason they rubbed your chest with Vicks when you had a cough at night, and put your feet in mercilessly hot water and wrapped you in blankets to sweat it out of you, when you should probably have had an ice bath.

My mother and father never talked about loving each other. It would be enough that every day of the last five years of my father's life, as he lay helpless in a hospital bed, my mother took a bus and a trolley car each way, winter and summer, to see him, whatever his mood, however little he might have to say.

Life was by no means a Norman Rockwell *Saturday Evening Post* cover. There were sad days, painful days, heartbreaking days. The scars remain, testimony that life here, all life here, is imperfect. But there were never days (and I don't think I'm unconsciously blocking them out) when we suspected that our mother and father didn't love us. Sometimes this love could hurt, bring tears, anger, resentment. But it could never be seriously questioned. There were too many obvious sacrifices made for us; and even more importantly, one that was not at all obvious then, but one I have come to learn is the most difficult sacrifice of all: to suffer *our* pain when they knew that we didn't think that *they* knew or cared that we were in pain.

Was it my good friend Elie Wiesel who said: "If you don't know what pains me, you don't really love me"? It's surprising now, and somehow comforting even these many years later, to recognize how very well my mother and father knew what pained each of us, at varying periods of our lives and accepted the sense of helplessness not only of being able to do little about our pain, but of knowing that we thought they *didn't* know, or care.

I'm writing as though I understand it all, when I don't. What I have come to believe, however, is that this is both an unerring proof of love and the inevitable price of love: to know what pains those one loves, to suffer their pain and to know that they *don't* know that you *do* know and *do* suffer with them. (That's about as convoluted a thing as I have ever said, and I wish I knew how to say it better, for I'm certain about it.)

Indeed, I doubt that there's a bishop in the world who doesn't know the pain of those who suffer because they find Church teaching difficult and who think their bishop neither knows of their suffering nor cares about it. Nor do I know of any bishops unaware of the built-in problems of family life, or the struggle many people have merely to survive, or the daily pains and sufferings of the ordinary lives of their people. Not that I patronize my own people here in the archdiocese thinking of them as children, except as we are all children of God. But when I look back on what demanded the greatest anguish of a set of parents who loved us beyond a doubt, I am sure that it was quite like that of so many bishops today, and most of all, that of the Bishop of Rome we call the pope.

Am I suggesting that we feel sorry for our bishops, including the Archbishop of New York? No more than I'm suggesting that my sisters and brother and I feel sorry for Thomas J. and Dorothy M. O'Connor, long since gone to God. They loved us. They wouldn't expect us to feel sorry for them for loving us, and paying the price.

Their Prayer-Watch Over the World

My mother was a world class non-sleeper. She would "rest her eyes" in a chair at night, with my father harassing her to "Go to bed, Dot." Dot would insist she wasn't asleep, but that if she was, that was *her* business, and if anybody should go to bed, *he* should. Whereupon he would sigh his martyr's sigh, shake his head and go back to reading the obituaries. He seemed to like to do that right before his night prayers. He took for granted that every night could well be his last. I suspect he wanted to see if there was anybody he knew in the obituaries that he might be meeting up with.

It was really my mother's prayer life, however, that did her in, as far as sleep was concerned, and that was the real reason she preferred a chair in the living room to going to bed. Once she made the move upstairs, she would have to kneel down and say her prayers, an exercise so extensive that, by her own account, it would " knock all the sleep" out of her. Not one prayerful *i* could be left undotted, not one pious *t* uncrossed, once she began.

I don't know how God computes these things, but if going

the distance counts, my mother was a marathon pray-er all the way. The Blessed Mother would get her Rosary, St. Rita of Cascia, whom she always credited with arranging the restoration of her sight, would get her novena. Somewhere along the line she did business with St. Thérèse of Lisieux.

In any event, it would be a long time till she would push herself up on her feet once more, to roam the house and look for the morning. The only time we realized that the years had begun to show on her was when we noticed her taking an occasional catnap during the day, in her living room chair, of course. You lie down in the daytime when you're sick. Period.

I'm sure they never discussed it, but my father prayed almost exclusively during daylight hours, as though he and my mother had divided between themselves a 24-hour watch over the world. At home, he was often an out-loud pray-er — the kind that drives some people crazy in church, when they have gone there for a little peace and quiet. In church, however, he prayed in silence, disturbing no one, except when you're supposed to pray out loud, then he *could* distract some by praying more slowly than anyone else in such fashion as to make others feel they were praying too fast, even while they felt annoyed at him. My father could absorb a lot of being annoyed at!

As my mother, my father was big on the Rosary, but equally big on a little prayer book worn to a frazzle from daily leafing. Prayerbook users are in a class by themselves. They pick up holy cards from funerals, ordinations, weddings and anniversaries, cut prayers out of newspapers and magazines, and if they've been at it long enough, even scribble a few homemade prayers of their own on the backs of pictures of their kids. Everything goes into the little prayer book, which eventually needs a half-dozen rubber bands to hold it together. I never knew which saints my father had struck up a special acquaintance with, until I went through his prayer book after he died: He was way ahead of me. He was clearly on a first name basis with saints I have never met.

I don't suppose that as things go many people might have

considered my father a great success, or my mother, either. He died an invalid, basically bedridden for his final five years, with literally nothing in the bank and not a penny under the mattress. My mother would have been puzzled if anyone asked her if she considered herself a success. She just kind of lived, and took care of my father. Of course, that was on top of taking care of the four of us kids.

As I reflect on the lives of these two remarkable people to whom I owe so much, I try to weigh them in terms of "success." It's not really difficult. I need only ask myself if, without their respective prayer-watches, the three of their kids who married would have married so happily, each for a lifetime, and the single one would have become a priest.

The Dazzling Value of One Soul

We probably do very few things in life for one, single reason. I'm sure a number of factors motivated me to become a priest. But I'm absolutely certain that if somewhere along the line I had not become convinced of the blinding value of the human soul, no other motive or collection of motives would have been enough. As many of my age, boys and girls, we looked at pictures, read magazines, saw occasional simple movies (they were much less common then, and certainly simple) about "the missions." We learned of Maryknoll sisters and priests through books like *When the Sorghum Was High*, of Columban brothers and priests through earlier counterparts of *The Red-Lacquered Gate*, of the Holy Ghost Fathers through pictures of snow-capped Kilimanjaro.

China became a dream we were driven to live, Africa a land of risks we had to take. We would do what all missionaries did: we would open medical clinics, cleanse the sores of lepers, feed the hungry, teach the illiterate, fight the lions of ignorance, slay the dragons of superstition. A great deal of it was romantic and sentimental, much of it unrealistic, as I was to learn years later in visiting many of the lands and peoples I had known only from what were then vast distances. But through it all ran one never-changing motif: we would "save souls." However naive we may have been about the real worlds of Shanghai and Nairobi, about the reason for going to such places and living out our lives among "our people," far, far from home and loved ones, about this reason we never doubted. We would become sisters, brothers, priests and save souls.

And what was that all about? That was all about having been taught and believing that Christ would have come into this world and suffered and died for one soul, had there been but one in the world. Such was the value of a human soul, we were taught. Such was the cost, the price Jesus paid, not to save "the world," but to save each one of us individually, so precious is each one of us to Him. And this is what we *had* to tell the peoples of Timbuktu and Mandalay and the Fiji Islands. And more than *telling* them, we had to love them in the same way and live and die for them, to help them save their souls.

Were we uncharitable? Were many of them better "Christians" than we were, even if they hadn't heard of Christ? Were their real needs radically different from those we dreamed of fulfilling? How do you calculate these things a half-century later?

Let whatever was real, whatever fantasy of a world long ago, the world of my boyhood missionary dreams, be sorted out by others. This I believe: Neither the value nor the cost of a human soul has changed. If I did not believe that passionately, I would see absolutely no point in being Archbishop of New York, no sense in being a priest at all.

The Archbishop of New York, as any sister, brother, priest, deacon, any layperson, married or single, has grave obligations to the poor, the hungry, the homeless, to all in need. That's of the essence of our religion. It drenches the Gospels. I am keenly aware that the unusual visibility and the extraordinary status given the Archbishop of New York require that, in addition, I concern myself sincerely with an almost endless number of "civic" problems, the general needs of the community, inside and outside our faith, the drug and alcohol problems, the prison problems, the AIDS problems, the housing problems, the racial problems, and countless more. I accept such opportunities as a great privilege. But in my heart of hearts, critical as are all of these needs, and grave as my obligations to help meet them are, for me there is an above and beyond and beneath, and that is my obligation and high, high privilege to try to help people save their souls. That's quite simply why I am a priest.

When I ask people to come home at Christmas, at Easter, or whenever, I am asking them to give up whatever it may be, however precious in their lives, that is keeping them from intimate union with our divine Lord; hence, risking their eternal salvation. I want those who have drifted to recover their mooring, those who have slipped and fallen to relearn the mercy of the Christ who came to earth to pick up the pieces of broken lives. I want every one who will find peace only by returning to Mass and the sacraments to find that peace. I want those who have rejected Church teaching to embrace it once again. But I want all this and more ultimately for one reason that transcends all others: that Christ died to pay for our salvation, that Christ suffered and died because of the dazzling value of each individual soul. Had only *you* been alive in all this world, He would have come and suffered and died for you.

"Think Small"

Even though I was only a 10-year-old altar boy, I was ashamed of the cakes my mother baked for card parties at St. Clement's, our parish church. They were smaller than any other kid's mother's cakes, and the icing wasn't nearly so gooey.

It wasn't until I felt guilty enough over being ashamed that I decided to give my mother a hearing. It was embarrassing to learn that she had known all along that I was ashamed of her cakes, and had decided she would let me live with my shame until I learned how little I knew.

Then she told me the secret — her cakes were packed with eggs. They cost twice as much as the bigger cakes made by the other kids' mothers and the parish could sell them for a lot more! My mother was a very classy lady, as dumb as several dozen foxes. She knew more than somewhat about 10-year-old kids. So did the priest who heard my confession. When I told him I was ashamed of my mother in front of other kids whose mothers baked bigger cakes for the parish, he asked me if I thought Jesus was ashamed of Mary because she didn't have Him born in a palace. I didn't quite see at the time what that had to do with the size of cakes, but since I can write about it more than a half-century later, it must have made an impression on me.

However I mixed up the lesson didn't matter. The priest in his way, my mother in hers, did something to what we would fancily call today my "value system."

First, I learned that mothers and priests are smarter than 10-year-old kids. I'm not sure everybody takes that for granted today, so I'm glad I learned it when I did.

Secondly, I learned that mothers are more important than cakes. I'm not sure that's taken for granted today, either. In fact, the more I thought about it, the more I discovered that my mother, in particular, was more important to me than even other kids' opinions, which at the age of 10 were practically the most important thing in the world.

The third thing I learned was picked up somewhere or other by some great big corporation a couple of decades later. Was it ITT? I don't remember. I remember only the ads in magazines: *Think Small!* I suppose the computer chip had been discovered, and the big move in communications and information-systems technology was toward packaging in tiny elements what once required huge pieces of equipment and cables, and so on.

Whatever the company was, I don't pretend it got the idea from me, but the minute I first saw the ad I thought: *That's what* my mother was teaching me. And it was one of the greatest things she ever taught me, she and the priest in the confessional.

Basically, they were telling me not to be fooled by appearances, especially in regard to people. Look at each individual person as a *person*, made in the Image of God. Look at each baby as the Christ Child. Think of every human being — black, white, brown, red, yellow, male, female, Latin, Russian, Korean, fat, thin, tall, short — think of every human person with awe, treat every human person with the respect, the reverence owed to the Most High God.

"Think small," my mother and the priest were telling me. Think of a tiny little manger — a very small manger in Bethlehem, a very small town, where the Son of the Most High God of all heaven and earth was born as a very small baby. Don't look at "masses" of people, nameless, faceless.

Don't think of "the poor," or "the homeless," or "the addicted." That wasn't my mother's way, or the mode of speech that reflected her thinking. In our house we talked about the poor family down the street, the retarded girl who lived catty-corner from us. There are no "poor," there are poor *persons*, homeless *persons*, there are *persons* ravaged by drugs.

Most of the persons in our lives when I was a kid — all of them, really — were little persons, unimportant as the world judges people. Nobody had any money. Nobody's name was ever in the newspapers. Had the Queen of England happened by, I imagine, with all due respect, that we would have been curious, but really wouldn't have thought her more *important* than the stevedore who lived next door to us.

I'm sure I didn't appreciate then what years of living have made very precious to me, this critical need to think small, which in essence results in treating everyone in the same way. I suspect it's why, when I visit persons with AIDS in our hospitals, I don't see a disease, I see persons — persons who once hoped and dreamed, and in some cases still do; persons who may have come from families very much like mine; persons in very deep anguish, very deep mental and spiritual pain. It's why I can see *persons* screaming with frustration in St. Patrick's Cathedral —*persons*, not mere demonstrators — and why I can't feel any bitterness toward them—only sadness despite the ridiculous headlines and even more ridiculous newspaper articles about an "angry O'Connor taut with rage," etc., etc., etc.

It's funny how I remembered that cake. After the sad events in St. Patrick's Cathedral, one of my lovely nieces was telling me how fascinating it is to be simultaneously a mother and a daughter. She's a terrific mother of three, herself, and was one of eight. She's surprised at how often she finds herself talking to her children precisely as her mother talked to her at their age, and having her wisdom questioned by her children precisely as she had questioned her mother's wisdom at their age. It tickled me, since her mother is my sister, and one of the great mothers of the century. She should be. She learned from a woman who knew a lot more than how many eggs to put into a cake.

The Beginning of Trust

Does every kid have an older sister who keeps telling him he's adopted? I sure did. She's the same one who told me on a late Christmas Eve that Santa Claus was downstairs in our kitchen with his whiskers caught in the gas range. That worried me a great deal. That I had allegedly been left in a basket on the front doorstep and taken into the family didn't worry me in the slightest. On the contrary, it made me feel special. In fact, I couldn't wait to tell my mother and father!

I remember the day I did. My father looked me right in the eye and put his hand on my little shoulder. His answer was as important to the rest of my life as anything I have ever heard since. "This is your mother, son, and I'm your father. You were born in the house. But if we *had* found you in a basket on the doorstep, we would have been proud to bring you in and love you as much as we do now." That's called security. I have always been grateful to my sister that she raised the question.

There's a difference now. I no longer have to think little-boy thoughts about what to get my father for Father's Day. I always offer Mass for him, of course, which he liked most when I was a young priest before he died. But apart from that, I spend much of the day grateful for what he gave *me*: the trust I felt in him that was the beginning of my trust in God. Of that, I am certain. I could always believe my father. He never told me less than the truth.

Recently I read a remark about myself by a newspaper reporter to the effect that I always seem to be absolutely certain about what I preach.

He's not far from the mark. When I preach the truths that the Church teaches, I am preaching what I believe with every bone in my body. They are not simply truths that I heard about in Church as a youngster, however, or was taught in a seminary.

My father *lived* the fundamental truths of the faith he taught me and nurtured and strengthened me in. He was skeptical about many things in life, including various politicians and an occasional bishop or priest. But if he ever had the vaguest doubt about Church *teaching*, he had to have been a greater actor than even Rex Harrison, for he sure fooled me.

That was why, when he said to me, "I'm your father, son," there wasn't the slightest doubt in my mind about my lineage. This was a man of truth.

I suppose that's the dominant characteristic of my sense of the Fatherhood of God: that He is a God of truth. I can trust Him. I can depend on what the Church teaches because it is His Son's Church, filled with the Spirit of truth. I don't have any problem with that at all. I feel deeply and sincerely sorry for those who do.

That can sound very smug and complacent. It isn't, because I know my faith is a pure gift from God, as my father was a pure gift from God. I am profoundly aware that I have done nothing to deserve either, but I am deeply grateful for both.

Anyway, how can you become all puffed up with yourself if

you have a sister who insists you were found in a basket on the doorstep? Who knows? Did even my father for once in his life juggle the truth?

The Mystery Carries Itself

My father never heard of St. Thomas Aquinas' five ways of demonstrating the existence of God. It was enough for him to know that nobody in the world was smart enough to explain how John McCormack's voice could come out through a crystal radio set. My father knew mystery when he saw it, and the mystery was infinitely more important to him than the music itself. Indeed, he never really heard a great deal of it all. He was busy marveling over the mystery.

Immanuel Kant found God in "the starry skies above me and the moral law within me." My father didn't read much Immanuel Kant of a Sunday afternoon, but when night would fall, out would come the "cat's whisker" to scratch away at the precious piece of crystal, and God was as close to him in the static as ever He was to Kant in the heavens and the law.

I'm writing this, I confess, propped up on my pillows in my bed, night prayers finished, Brahms' Fourth rolling over me, mysteriously, ever so mysteriously. I'm nostalgic. Tomorrow I'll have my Mass, my wonderful, mysterious Mass, in what I know will be a packed cathedral at 8:30 in the morning. Even now I'm not fully certain what I'll preach, the substance is there, but the finishing touches will have to wait till I sense the mood of the morning in these troubled times. Then I'll spend an hour before the Mystery of the Holy Sacrament in the tabernacle of our little chapel before going into the great Cathedral of St. Patrick, assured without doubt that the Mystery again will overcome me as so often in the past, and I will preach the Word given me, with malice toward none, with charity toward all.

My father would have liked the question St. Patrick put to

himself, liked and understood it: "How did so great and salutary a gift come to me, the gift of knowing and loving God. . . ?" Nor would my father have thought it strange to ask that question while probing with the cat's whisker, trying to find Richard Crooks singing "Macushla," and far more often than not failing in the effort, but thrilling with the mystery of it all, nonetheless.

That's why, I suppose, I work on my preaching, but I don't worry about it. The Mystery carries itself, every time. And it will carry me and all of us through tomorrow, no matter what happens. It is, after all, the Mystery of the Holy Faith, the same that made a saint of Patrick, who, for all his fame, would have died a poor pagan without it.

Father Murphy, Two Mothers and Two Sons

Every time I go through Philadelphia by train, I think of Father John Murphy. The train passes very close to my old home parish of St. Clement, where many years ago Father Murphy was what we then called a curate and my brother, Tom, was in about the sixth grade of the parish school.

This time I was praying the Office of Vespers for the next day's Feast of the Triumph of the Holy Cross, followed the day after by the Feast of Our Lady of Sorrows. All the more reason for thinking of Father Murphy, and the cross he had to share with not one mother, but with two.

My mother had been waiting for my older brother to come home from school, about a mile away. When the doorbell rang it was Father Murphy not young Tom. She was surprised, but had no reason to be alarmed. Then she noted that poor Father Murphy was whiter than the proverbial ghost and shaking as though he had seen one.

"I don't know how to tell you this, Mrs. O'Connor. It's terrible. Your son Thomas was killed crossing the railroad track on his way home from school."

My mother neither screamed nor fainted.

Father Murphy was astounded by her calm and the perplexity on her face, as she stared over his shoulder. He was certain she either couldn't have understood, or had gone into a state of shock, or simply didn't want to believe what he had told her. He couldn't see what she could — young Tom coming across the street whistling, school books over his shoulder. Father Murphy turned and saw him, too.

How wonderful for everyone had the story ended there. The suffering was to get worse as the truth stabbed the curate in the middle of the stomach. There were two Thomas O'Connors in St. Clement's School. He had yet another mother to confront, and this time her son would not come whistling across the street.

I finished praying Vespers. The whole story of Father Murphy, two mothers and two sons had flashed through my memory in a fraction of the time it has taken me to write of it, but it lingered all the way to New York. I thought of the countless occasions on which I have had to do what Father Murphy had to do, perhaps as painful as anything a priest ever has to do. What "formula" can there be for conveying the word of the death of a beloved, especially if the death is sudden and totally unexpected? Who can pretend not to feel utterly helpless in the face of the awesome emptiness in the heart of the one suffering the loss? Yet at that same moment the priest knows that he is inexpressibly privileged to be sharing the overpowering sense of helplessness on the part of one suffering the loss, and to know that it is the helplessness of Christ on the cross, of Mary beneath the cross.

Nor is saying that to mouth a "formula," but to feel at first hand the Mystery of Faith. Christ *was* helpless. Christ *was* empty and desolate. Christ *did* make possible the salvation of the world by dying. And I can not believe that Mary wasn't sobbing her heart out as she watched and shared her son's helplessness.

I doubt that any priest ever feels quite the sense of intimacy that he feels in sharing the all-engulfing suffering of another human being. Perhaps it's as close as we can come to "feeling" the union of the human and the divine in Christ.

Father Murphy was a long time ago. I couldn't have been more than 5 or 6 years old, perhaps the age when little boys remember most.

Mary and the Saints

The Blessed Virgin Mary:
Mary's Going to Do It for Us

It was probably the best vacation I have ever had. There were 60 of us, in all, 59 nuns and myself! We spent the whole week talking about Mary.

I had the easy job; I conducted the retreat. They did all the work; they listened. That's what it was, of course, a retreat, at our seminary, St. Joseph's, in the Dunwoodie section of Yonkers. The sisters came from all over the archdiocese, from a variety of religious communities. A number were young and sprightly; more than one or two used canes. But from youngest to oldest they radiated goodness and holiness. I felt like the only reprobate in the lot. I have conducted retreats for women religious before, but this one was different. We called it a "Marian" Retreat. I make no secret of the fact that even after all these years of devotion to Mary, I really had to dig into the Sacred Scriptures, read everything I could lay my hands on and think and pray up a storm before I felt ready to conduct the retreat. Even then, I really didn't feel ready. I felt I had to begin by telling the sisters I would be stumbling along, trying to work my way through it.

But the great thrill that the retreat turned out to be had nothing to do with anything I said. It had everything to do with the power of Mary and the openness of the sisters to her influence. Mary revealed insights into her life that I, for one, had experienced only inadequately before — the suffering in her role as a widow, the perplexity of being a "single parent," the pain of losing her child, the bewilderment of trying to understand that child, the horror of seeing that child in his full manhood on a cross, the deep, deep grief of putting his body in a tomb.

I suspect, however, that what most overwhelmed us all, was the deepening of our recognition — however dim — of the indispensability of Mary in God's entire plan and salvation. Clearly, if I had been thinking and praying enough during the years, it wouldn't have hit me like the proverbial ton of bricks. But

I must confess that, although I had a kind of vague theological understanding of Mary's importance, it was something "way out there" — that without Mary's saying "I will" to the angel, Christ might very well not have come into the world. I had thought about that off and on through the years, but it had never moved me quite so personally, even though I had preached it to others. Or maybe it had, but so much that goes with that thought has eluded me through the years. It was only during the retreat, as I went back and forth from the Old Testament to the New, back and forth from the prophecies about Mary and Jesus to the fulfillment of those prophecies; it was only when I was struck time after time with God's meticulous care in preparing Mary to conceive and nourish His Son in her womb, and to be in exactly the right place at exactly the right time, that the full realization of how much depended on her really got through to me.

Scrap all that, if you will. Say it doesn't really matter anyway, except to an historian, but I'll challenge you every inch of the way. For what jumped out at me during the retreat was not simply the role Mary did play, but the role she does play. After so many years as a priest, each day during the retreat I became more conscious of the fact that Mary is as indispensable to my life as she was to Christ's. There is simply no way I can get along without her and be a whole person, mentally, emotionally, morally or physically. That's not just a pious cliché. That's a very hard reality.

The clearer this became during the retreat, the clearer became the understanding that many attacks on Mary are really attacks on the Church. Destroy devotion to Mary and you destroy fidelity to the Church. I know that sounds terribly exaggerated and grossly oversimplified. Maybe before I conducted this Marian Retreat I would have thought so, too. That's the point: you have to steep yourself in thinking about Mary, reading and talking about her, praying to her and through her, for long enough and intensely enough to get caught up in it all. Then the light breaks through.

Of course, I had 59 helpers, each one of whom saw the light before I did, I'm sure. Maybe you think you have seen people pray before, or respond to the Holy Spirit before, but I'll eat at least a half-dozen of the hats constantly being given me if you have seen anything like the praying and the responding of 59 nuns. I thought they would begin to glow in the dark before the retreat was over.

In any event, the retreat *did* end, but I will be amazed if the new-found sense of Mary's presence and her indispensability in this 20th century will fade for a long, long time, if at all. Mary came too close to each of us, and she made clear that she wants to come at least as close to everyone in the Archdiocese of New York. As a matter of fact, that's another thing — a big thing — that made the retreat different. We seemed to find ourselves making it for the entire archdiocese. So many of our prayers were for the archdiocese, for our sisters, our priests and brothers and laypersons. We talked so much about the work of the archdiocese, about its role in the Church Universal. We talked and meditated and prayed a great deal, indeed about what it means to be a sister, a brother, a priest, a dedicated layperson quite explicitly here in this archdiocese.

Mary is going to revitalize the archdiocese. I truly believe she is going to give us new courage to fight pornography, to reduce the terrifying number of abortions, to strengthen marriages and families, to give our young people the power they need to overcome the terrible pressures and temptations they experience, to win thousands of lonely and weak and alienated Catholics back to Mass and the sacraments, to feed our hungry and house our homeless and rid ourselves of racism, and to restore, above all, a deep, abiding sense of reverence for every human person, each one as precious and as sacred to Mary as the Son who was flesh of her flesh and blood of her blood.

Fifty-nine nuns can sure make a believer out of an archbishop!

St. Elizabeth Ann Seton:
Lovely Lady of New York

Friends skilled in communications tell me I should not scratch my head while on television. They call it a sign of perplexity and they don't want me to appear perplexed about anything. They want me to appear very certain about everything. They may be right except that I am often perplexed on television and off. However, my head itches more frequently when I'm on television. I suspect it's the heat of the lights.

At any rate, I was quite perplexed, and I know I didn't scratch my head, because I had my miter on, that tall, pointed hat that I think at least makes me look solemn, if not smart. It's scratch-proof. My perplexity concerned New York's attitude, or lack of attitude, toward Elizabeth Ann Bayley Seton.

Elizabeth Seton was the first person (and the only one, to date) born in what was to become the United States (the year was 1774) to be canonized a saint of the Roman Catholic Church. Moreover, she was a woman. And she was born right here in New York, where her house still stands.

Why is there so little excitement about her in New York? That's what perplexes me.

Elizabeth Seton is the Mother Seton who founded the Sisters of Charity. They were the first religious community in New York, established the first Catholic hospital, the first Catholic asylum, the first Catholic girls' secondary school, and on and on and on. They have been, and are, invaluable to New York — and I mean New York not only the Archdiocese of New York. But they are only one "branch" of Mother Seton's sisters, who can be found all over the country and beyond.

Elizabeth Ann Bayley Seton was not canonized, however, for founding the Sisters of Charity, as valuable an achievement as that was. She was canonized because she was an extraordinarily, remarkably heroic and holy woman. She loved her husband very much. He died of tuberculosis before she was 30 and left her penniless with five children. She loved her children very much. Three of them died and another came close to breaking her heart. She loved her friends very much, the high society of the day into which she had been born — the social set that included George Washington. They rejected her, ridiculed her, despised her — because she became a Roman Catholic. Her husband's fortune had been lost before he died; now her aunt disinherited her.

She opened a school to support her children, eventually went to Baltimore and from there by covered wagon to Emmitsburg, Maryland, where now her body rests in an elegant chapel, surrounded fittingly by Sisters of Charity.

What can a bare-bones sketch say of this woman so gentle, so beautiful, with the courage of a lioness? I believe I know something of her as a widowed mother because my beloved sister is a widowed mother whose marriage to Hugh was as joyous as Elizabeth's to William. I think I know something of her, too, from the unmarried women I know who resist the pressures to abort babies conceived without husbands, and struggle heroically to support such babies in a hostile society. The lonely, courageous divorced women I know, who struggle to retain their integrity and maintain their faith in a world that would devour them — these, too, I'm sure teach me something of Elizabeth Seton. I am certain I know her as a religious, because I see her every day in the patient, self-sacrificing sisters with whom I work and whom I have the privilege to serve as their bishop.

In fact, I suspect I have come to know Elizabeth Ann Bayley Seton rather well — well enough to wish that a lot more New Yorkers would make her acquaintance. She was all woman, all gentleness, all passion and dedication and courage, all suffering, all saint. The more I think about it the more I recognize that I have a serious obligation to introduce as many New Yorkers to this lovely lady as I can. At the moment I'm not sure how, so I'm scratching my head, but I'll bet Elizabeth Ann Bayley Seton's Sisters of Charity will find a way.

St. Valentine:
I Tell You, Young Lovers

Who has to learn about love from the birds? I checked with more than one book about saints to try to figure out the relationship between St. Valentine and Valentine's Day. I might better have consulted a book on ornithology. The saint books tell me Geoffrey Chaucer observed that birds mate on Feb. 14, the day on which St. Valentine was martyred some 1070 years before Chaucer was born!

Figure that out. The story goes that having observed the birds courting, young men and women decided it was a good idea. And if Feb. 14 was good enough for a birdly exchange of affection, it should be good enough for human beings, in which case they might as well call upon the saint of the day to assure good luck in the draw.

Now to me that's like telling Virginia there's no Santa Claus. No — worse: it's like telling Virginia that St. Nicholas was a myth, the Church's effort to capitalize on the legend of Santa Claus. Why do we do things like that?

Why don't we jump right into the real story of St. Valentine? In other words, why not begin at the beginning, recognize St. Valentine as the lover that he was, and see how readily he could become the symbol of love for young and old alike for a good, solid 17 centuries, with no sign of weakening.

Valentine was a Roman and a priest. He loved people enough that he got himself arrested for helping prisoners. Under arrest, he was asked to bear allegiance to Jupiter and Mercury. He loved Jesus enough to denounce both Roman gods as frauds, and despicable frauds, at that. Recalling Jesus before Pilate, he seized the teachable moment to proclaim his Christian faith. While awaiting judgment, he was placed in the hands of Asterius, lieutenant to Calpurnius, Prefect of Rome, who had to do the judging.

The plot thickened more than somewhat when Asterius, whose adopted young daughter had been blind for two years, told

Valentine: "If you restore her sight, I'll believe in Jesus Christ." From all accounts, Valentine had never tried anything like that before, but he had no difficulty in reflecting on Jesus' cure of a blind man. Nor was it hard for him to remember Jesus' admonition to His disciples, that if they truly believed, nothing was impossible to them. He truly believed. He placed his hands on the youngster's eyes, prayed to Jesus, Light of the World, and the little girl saw as bright as day. The father kept his word and the entire family was baptized. Valentine is reported as being more than happy, but rather less than surprised.

The Roman emperor, on the contrary, was less than happy and rather more than surprised that a Roman army officer would betray the Roman gods. In order to cover up the miracle, he had Asterius and his entire family put to death. A thoroughgoing beating was administered to Valentine, but he couldn't see giving up the Love of his life, so they finally put him to death, by beheading him. The story concludes with the matronly Sabinilla taking the dead Valentine to her estate, and burying him with reverence. Less than a hundred years later Pope Julius I, an extraordinarily astute and highly orthodox pope, built a basilica over the burial spot. Destroyed in the seventh century, it nonetheless became a popular shrine for pilgrims for a long and happy time thereafter.

I like that story. Whatever little adornments may have been added through the centuries — (Is the little blind girl too coincidental, for example?) — it's the story of your basic martyr. The Church knew thousands upon thousands of them in its early centuries, more than a few ripped to shreds by lions for the amusement of the crowds. Through the centuries, legions of martyrs have given their lives — some, as Valentine, their heads, as well. Peter was crucified, Paul beheaded, Ignatius devoured by lions. Agnes and Agatha were tortured and their bodies mutilated before they were put to death. In a later age, Thomas More and John Fisher would lose their heads at the whim of Henry VIII. In yet a later age, missionaries to Japan would be crucified, and priests in Mexico would be hanged by the neck until dead, or executed by firing squad. Still later, Maria Goretti was stabbed to death.

These were *real* lovers, these men and women. The words of the Master were crystal clear: "Greater love than this no one has, than to lay down his life for his friends."

Now this is why I ask: Who has to learn about love from the birds? Why couldn't a young couple have been friends of Father Valentine, have known him as an exceptionally holy man, been torn up over his death, recognized that he died out of love, and placed their own love under his protection? I can imagine, for example, that one of them might have been the daughter of Sabinilla and the other the son of Calpurnius. Why not? They could have told their friends about it at their wedding, when they were laying down their own lives for each other. The word would have spread quickly, outlasted the ages, and turn out to be a bonanza for Hallmark. Makes a lot more sense to me than the story of the birds.

I kid a lot, but I'm very serious about this: the martyrs have played a crucial role in my own love life. Learning about many of them when I was a lad kindled a love of my faith that has never diminished. Hearing stories of their love for men and women and children of every land — a love that literally drove them to their deaths — I had little difficulty in hearing the voice that called me to the priesthood and to love everyone I meet, as an image of God. Pondering the love that never flinched before an axe or a cross, before a hangman's noose or the jaws of a lion, before arrows or muskets, stirred up in my own soul a love of Christ — I say without embarrassment or vanity — that I know will sustain me till the day I die, and for everlasting eons into eternity.

So I tell you, young lovers, whoever you are, and old lovers, just as well: If you want to learn about *real* love, St. Valentine is your man. He loved when it hurt, and that's the only kind of love that lasts.

St. Teresa of Avila:
Thoughts on a Visit to Avila

The Spanish was absolutely flawless, but the face was unmistakably American. What in the world was she doing here in Avila, in the most famous convent in the western world? I was on my way to Santiago de Compostela and the tomb of St. James the Apostle, in the northwest corner of Spain. Avila was the perfect place to stop to offer Mass. All my life I had been in awe of St. Teresa of Avila, contemplative Carmelite, mystic, thoroughgoing woman, friend of St. John of the Cross.

The 16th century was as turbulent as any age the Church has known. Born in 1515, Teresa inherited the whirlwind of the Protestant Reformation and lived through the years of the Church's own internal reformation, the Council of Trent. By every human measure of reckoning, she should have been completely obscured by the events of the day, not even a footnote in Church history. Instead, she dominated events with her courage, her common sense, her poverty, and her deep, deep spirituality.

Teresa was born at Avila, in a family of Castilian aristocrats. At 14, she was a beauty, with a 14-year-old's fascination for fashions, fads and romantic fantasies. An illness that was to plague her throughout her life, possibly malignant malaria, turned her mind to the reading of the Letters of St. Jerome, and she convinced her very reluctant father that she should become a Carmelite.

The Carmel of the Incarnation which Teresa initially entered, however, was hardly famous for its austerity. Nuns of "good family" had their servants, visitors were abundant, solitude and poverty were taken very casually, at best. Teresa tried — she tried for 25 years — then she begged and pleaded and finally "demanded" authority to establish a house where she and her associates, 13 of them, could practice solitude, prayer, poverty and the kind of austerity she passionately believed she was called to. The permission finally came, and she established not one but

17 such convents, which served as models of reform for religious life everywhere.

Repeated returns of her illness, her self-imposed austerities, and difficulties in prayer were minor sufferings in comparison with the opposition to reform that finally provoked the prayer: "Lord, how true it is that whoever works for you is paid in troubles."

It's ironic that St. Teresa of Avila is often called "big Teresa," as distinct from St. Thérèse, the "Little Flower," who was to follow her as a Carmelite over three centuries later. As a youngster, I pictured "big Teresa" as gargantuan! She was actually a beautiful lady, as charming and affectionate as she was spiritually tough and courageous. There's a portrait of her at Avila, done by a monk of her day (a Friar Juan de la Miseria). Painted in 1570, it presents an unmistakably handsome woman. More famous, however, is the Bernini sculpture in Rome, in the Church of Santa Maria della Vittoria. Bernini obviously saw her as very thoroughly feminine, and sculpted her as such.

To see the tiny writing desk she used to produce such marvels on prayer and contemplation as *The Interior Castle*, to see the cell in which she lived and worked and wrote and prayed, in heat without air-conditioning and cold without fuel, embarrassed me quite as much as I prefer to be embarrassed. As I write these very words at 5 in the morning, I look around my toasty room (it's cold outside), at my book-lined walls and my reclining chair, and I ask myself if I even begin to understand the spiritual life!

I didn't ask *her*, but the beautiful American Carmelite in Avila, who opened the door for me and who spoke such lovely Spanish, with only the faintest trace of California, very possibly asked herself the same question when she first visited Avila as a tourist. Whether she asked it or not, she answered it, and came back to spend her life there.

It was as devout a Mass as I have ever offered, although I suspect I'll feel much the same when I offer Mass this week in our own seminary for the women contemplatives of the archdiocese, when they and I will meet to reflect together. Some of them will be Carmelites, others Redemptoristines, Dominicans, Sacramentines, Poor Clares, Missionaries of Charity, Maryknollers, Good Shepherd Sisters. All will be contemplative, all very holy women, all great gifts to the Archdiocese of New York. I will feel very humble among them.

St. Joseph: "How Is Your Mother, Son?"

It was the quality of my father's prayer that impressed me as a child, as a young man and in these years of my own aging. He could concentrate extraordinarily while fingering his beads. He wouldn't simply say "Hail Mary," he would virtually cry out to her, pleading for her help. Every Rosary was prayed as if it were to be his last.

I never saw my father with his mother, whose name, of course, was Mary, but I always suspected that when he called to the Mother of God it was in the same voice he used when, as a little boy, he had called to his own mother. There was a kind of childish plea in his prayer, even when breathed, as it sometimes was, in a weary old man's sigh.

I write on the first day of May, the feast of St. Joseph the Worker. My father's Rosaries were inevitably conscious of Joseph, as my father was inevitably conscious of being a worker. He was proud that Joseph had worked with his hands as he, himself, worked proudly with his hands. Naturally, to be a boy in our family was to be called Joseph. My father was Thomas Joseph as is my older brother. I am John Joseph. My brother who died was just plain Joseph. The carpenter father of Jesus was very special in our house.

It was after I conducted a retreat for priests and spoke of Joseph, that my priest friend, Father Joseph Kennedy, gave me a haunting poem of Sister Mary Ida's about Joseph and Mary. My

father was entranced by it. In some humble but secretly proud
way, I imagine, he saw his own mother in it, and himself. Don't ask
me how; just remember he was an Irishman with mystical feelings
deep in his bones.

The poem is called "Limbo." It begins:

> The Ancient Greyness shifted
> Suddenly and thinned
> Like mist upon the moors
> Before a wind.
> An old, old prophet lifted
> A shining face and said:
> "He will be coming soon.
> The Son of God is dead;
> He died this afternoon."
> A murmurous excitement stirred
> All souls.
> They wondered if they dreamed —
> Save one old man who seemed
> Not even to have heard.

The poem goes on, then, to talk about Moses and David and
all the others who had gone before Christ, wondering how they
could best welcome Him. Then suddenly:

> And there He was
> Splendid as the morning sun and fair
> As only God is fair.
> And they, confused with joy,
> Knelt to adore
> Seeing that He wore
> Five crimson stars
> He never had before.
> No canticle at all was sung.
> None toned a psalm, or raised a greeting song.
> A silent man alone

Of all that throng
Found tongue —
Not any other.
Close to His heart
When the embrace was done
Old Joseph said
"How is Your Mother,
How is Your Mother, Son?"

St. John Fisher and St. Thomas More: Two Who Wouldn't Say Wrong Was Right

I am in Rome on my *onomastico*, my name day.

It's not what brought me here, but it's a great day to be here. In Rome, one's name day, the feast of one's patron saint, is more important than one's birthday.

My patron saint is John Fisher, celebrated on June 22, together with St. Thomas More because they both had their heads chopped off by the same king, for the same reason. They both denied that the king could be the supreme head of the English Church and refused to take an oath that he could. Both were sentenced to life imprisonment in the Tower of London and the loss of their earthly goods. John Fisher was Bishop of Rochester; Thomas More had been Chancellor of England.

Both Fisher and More fell from the king's grace not because they took it upon themselves, either one, to attack his illicitly divorcing his wife and invalidly marrying another. They did not attack him at all. The problem developed when the king insisted that they support what he had done. Indeed, it is quite possible that neither the bishop nor the chancellor would have said a word, had Henry VIII not tried to force them into becoming accomplices in his villainy. He wanted them to declare that what they knew to be wrong was right. It was their refusal to prostitute either their consciences or the logic of the obvious that infuriated the king.

It is always that way. Lord Acton's axiom seems never to be proved false: "All power corrupts; absolute power corrupts absolutely." When the ruler makes up his own rules, in defiance of all convention and tradition, blatantly rejecting common sense norms of morality, demanding ordinary people to accept as right on his authority what their own intuition tells them is wrong, that ruler has been corrupted by his own sense of power. It happened to most of the Caesars. It happened to Napoleon Bonaparte. It happens every day, all over the world.

As all power corrupts, so every act of corruption must justify itself. Not content with handling his marital affairs to suit himself despite Fisher's and More's lack of support, Henry VIII was determined to institutionalize his "right" to do as he pleased. He would do that by arguing that neither the pope in Rome nor his representatives in England had any real authority over the Catholic Church in England, except that granted by the king himself, who must be recognized as supreme in every sphere.

Even in the face of *this* claim, Bishop Fisher and Chancellor More might have remained silent, had Henry not tried to force them to sign the "Supremacy Oath." It was *this* refusal that led to their imprisonment and eventual execution, rather than their failure to support the king's moral profligacy — but no one was fooled. The move to have himself declared supreme spiritual power was prompted by Henry's determination to justify his marital infidelities by asserting that he, and only he, had the supreme right to declare what was right, what was wrong.

To believers of the Genesis story, or of what it implies, this was precisely the sin of Adam. He would become God. He would determine for himself what is right, what is wrong. Eating forbidden fruit is always risky; calling forbidden fruit *permissible* is simply to deceive oneself. Poisoned fruit can still kill you no matter how much you try to convince yourself that you are eating an ordinary apple.

It's a terribly hot day in Rome, this my *onomastico*. The sirocco is blowing from North Africa across the Mediterranean, carrying unwelcome humidity that makes for sleepless nights and weary days. I think of the same date, the end of June, more than four and a half centuries ago, 1535 to be exact. It must have been terribly hot and humid in the Tower of London, and a thousand times worse on the scaffold, when the might that tried to make right severed the head from the shoulders of Bishop John Fisher, so recently appointed a cardinal in his prison cell. His blood took the place of the red hat Henry prohibited from being delivered to him. He did without it very well. It would have looked awfully strange atop his severed head that Henry caused to be exhibited on a pike for all the world to jeer at.

But the world finally claimed Cardinal Fisher's body, to entomb it, to honor it, to this very day.

St. John Fisher and St. Thomas More, who refused to prostitute their consciences or the logic of the obvious, are remembered with much greater admiration than the king who cut off their heads.

St. Blase:
Coleman's Mustard and St. Blase

For an Irishman, my father's faith in Coleman's English Mustard was amazing. Only the powder would do for his favorite winter sport: making mustard plasters. Two sheets of thin muslin were required and just enough water to turn the dry mustard into a scalding hot plaster, not too much water, lest the heat be dissipated. And to be applied to the chest — invariably mine — only after an equally scalding hot bath. This, of course, is to say nothing of the fiery fumes raging through my mouth, my nostrils, my eyes. The fumes seemed to be an essential part of the exercise.

That my chest bears even a scrap of skin today is a miracle for which my father deserves no credit. That I still have even a scrap of faith is an even greater miracle, for which my father deserves all the credit in the world except for what goes to my mother.

Oh, it was not the double scalding I took every time I had a sore throat that tested my faith. It was that despite my inevitable winter sore throats accompanied by the equally inevitable scaldings, they still trotted me off every year to the Feast of St. Blase to have my throat blessed between two candles. I can hear that priest today, rumbling: "Through the intercession of St. Blase, Bishop and Martyr, may God free you from ailments of the throat and from every other evil, in the Name of the Father and of the Son and of the Holy Ghost." Yes, Holy Ghost, and even though it was in Latin, I knew what was up. So why did my father always keep the English Mustard handy?

It took me a lot of years before I could face that faith-shattering contradiction fearlessly enough to discover the truth, which is undoubtedly that my father's mustard plasters would have killed me were it not for the intercession of St. Blase. So the throat blessing worked after all, in its own way!

I'm kidding, of course, because every year, on the 3rd of February, Feast of St. Blase, I, myself, am the priest who blesses innumerable throats in the cathedral with candles blessed the day before, on the Feast of the Presentation of the Infant Jesus in the Temple. And I say the same words but now in English. And one of the other priests or bishops celebrating Mass with me blesses my throat after I bless his.

I still get sore throats, although rarely any more, but now I gargle with salt water and confine Coleman's English Mustard to baked ham. So what is St. Blase all about, and why go through a ritual that doesn't seem to work? Superstition? Mumbo-jumbo? A good question, but it has a good, if not a simple answer.

As with any other blessing, the blessing of throats is a *sacramental*, not a sacrament and certainly not magic. Its primary purpose is spiritual — to bestow grace on the one blessed, and only when the blessed receives the blessing with faith and confidence. When I have my throat blessed I don't at all take for granted that if sore it will get better, or that it will never get sore again. But I *do* take for granted that if I really *need* a miracle (and I don't need a miracle when salt water or antibiotics will do the trick), I believe that it *can* happen, through the grace of God. What I *do* take for granted also is that, if I am properly disposed, I will be strengthened *spiritually* by the blessing, and maybe even be able to hold my tongue when I get angry and uncharitable, which for me is at least a minor miracle every time I succeed, and quite plausibly attributable in part to having my vocal chords blessed.

Nor do I ever discount for a moment that someone with, let us say, incurable cancer of the throat could be cured. Our God is a great God, and the Spirit breathes where the Spirit wills to breathe.

But who is to say that the hundreds of thousands everywhere who have their throats blessed on the Feast of St. Blase aren't spiritually enriched? Even the act of humility which brings a millionaire to the same set of candles as a pauper, for the same blessing, has to have a wealth of merit on its own.

Who was this bishop and martyr called Blase, and why single him out for the blessing? As with many of the saints of the early Church (Blase died in 316) about whom we know little except that they were very holy men and women — Blase was a martyr, and that's real holiness — legends abound, many of them delightful. We do know that he was the bishop of Sebaste in Armenia, where persecution of Christians raged even after freedom of worship was authorized in the Roman Empire. The story goes that Blase was forced to flee, lived as a hermit in a cave, and made friends with wild animals. Supposedly he was discovered by hunters who hauled him off to prison. En route, the story has it, a mother brought her son who was choking to death over a fishbone caught in his throat. Blase said a prayer, made the sign of the cross, and the bone was dislodged.

When Blase refused to sacrifice to pagan idols, he was beaten. When he refused again he was hanged from a tree, his flesh was torn with iron combs like those used by wool combers, and he was beheaded. There are variations on the story but that's it, in essence. In time, devotion spread throughout the world and the custom we now practice of blessing throats on his feast day came into being. An added note: the candles used are fixed into an X position, that of the St. Andrew Cross, the cross on which Andrew the Apostle, brother of Peter, the first pope, is said to have been crucified.

Why candles at all? One story is that when Blase was in a dungeon-like prison, the mother of the boy whose life had been saved brought him food and candles to see by. It is hard not to notice, however, that the day before the Feast of St. Blase is called Candlemas Day, when the candles are actually blessed. That's the day on which Mary and Joseph presented the infant Jesus, four days after His birth, to the prophet Simeon, in the Temple, and Simeon called the Christ Child "a light of revelation to the Gentiles." Years later, the custom developed of carrying lamps in procession on that feast day, representing Christ as the Light of the world. The candle, of course, is a beautiful symbol of Christ, who burned Himself out in the service of His Father for our salvation.

It all goes to make up this wondrous faith of ours which is at least as much mystery as it is knowledge, and more often than not a mix of each. As the Letter to the Hebrews puts it, "To have faith is to be sure of the things we hope for, to be certain of the things we cannot see." It's the faith to which I will be grateful to my mother and father all the days of my life, the faith that made it possible for me to reconcile mustard plasters with the blessing of throats, the faith that I may not live fully enough, but which I love ever so deeply. And on days like the Feast of St. Blase, I'm reminded of the countless numbers who have died for that faith, and I'm glad to be in church on their feast days, to think about them, to hope that some of their goodness will rub off on me. Even that is a good reason to get my throat blessed just to hobnob with St. Blase and be blessed through his intercession. As the blessing itself says, deliverance from *every* evil is asked, so even if my throat does bother me there are a lot more important evils I'd be happy to get rid of.

And whatever else, with the help of Coleman's English Mustard my father gave me a very healthy respect for Hell. If St. Blase does nothing but remind me of the same, it's worth putting my throat between the candles.

St. Ann and St. Joachim:
To Be a Grandparent . . .

It was an ever-so-much-simpler day, that first summer when I was a shiny new priest. Neither my mother, nor my father, nor I had ever set foot outside the United States, and here we were on pilgrimage to the Shrine of Ste. Anne de Beaupré, in Quebec. The train was summer-hot and pilgrim-packed from Philadelphia to Montreal, but cost next to nothing, included a steamer up the St. Lawrence to Quebec, a night in the famous Hotel Frontenac, and I was a pilgrimage chaplain! Difficult though it may be for regular participants in my St. Patrick's Cathedral Masses to believe, I had a bit of a voice in those days and no shame in encouraging others to belt out "On the Sidewalks of New York," which I had never trod at the time, "Take Me Out to the Ball Game," and a related repertoire familiar to citizens of the day who didn't know they were senior citizens. They just liked to sing, and we pulled into Montreal on the 133rd rendition of "Daisy, Daisy," alternating with "Home on the Range."

I was so fond of my mother and father on that simple trip, and so pleased to please them, particularly since to please me, my mother, scared to death of the water, had nonetheless agreed to go aboard the steamer to Quebec. What a beautiful trip. They had the kind of stateroom they had only seen in the movies, the food was lavish and exquisite, they were treated as royalty by fellow pilgrims as the mother and father of a priest, especially the priest who led the singing.

Forewarned, we weren't the slightest bit put off by the "commercialism" surrounding the shrine of St. Ann. Vendors go where crowds go. Further, we were wide-eyed over the shrine itself. My father had always kept a little bronze statue of St. Ann. That was my introduction to St. Ann, the statue that is now mine, but I had never really thought of her as a real person before, and certainly I had never thought of her as Jesus' grandmother, or of her husband as Jesus' grandfather. I remember being almost shocked by the idea, but then getting misty-eyed. Jesus with a

grandmother, a grandfather! And now, every time I see a grandparent holding a little grandchild so lovingly, I think of that day
in Quebec.

It was a highlight of our pilgrimage, but there was another,
the ride up the Saguenay River, beneath overhanging caves, to the
little Indian village of Tadoussac. The river was a silken ribbon,
the violinist a magician, the statue of Our Lady in a cleft of the
rocks exquisite, the singing of the *Ave Maria* ethereal. Would it all
be too trite today? Be it so, I will never forget or regret.

It all comes upon me each feast of SS. Ann and Joachim, each
July 26, when I am especially vulnerable to memories. My mother
and father became grandparents many times over, with no help
from me, but with a great deal of help from my sisters and brother,
who are now themselves grandparents immensely important to
their grandchildren. I don't know what today's sociologists would
have to say about it, but I do know that the many toddlers and
youngsters who have populated our clan would have missed
something indescribably valuable had they not known their grandparents.

I wish Ann and Joachim were a bit better known in the
United States. We do have our local churches in honor of one or the
other and a shrine here and there. But I don't recall a shrine
anywhere specifically honoring them as the grandparents of
Jesus, hence as a model and source of joy for all grandparents
everywhere. After all, if every baby, born and unborn, is fashioned
after Jesus, to be a grandparent is no small honor, nor an honor that
should be ignored.

St. Peter:
The Chair of Peter

There are chairs and there are chairs. The little wooden chair
I have in my bedroom has never been sat in. It's obviously there
to hold books, shoes, trousers — the flotsam and jetsam probably

piled on, hung on, thrown over countless chairs of its type in countless bedrooms in countless homes in New York and countless other cities, villages, towns and hamlets across the world. But there is only one Chair of St. Peter, and I'm determined to write about it on this very day the Church celebrates it, the 22nd day of February.

I rarely enter the great Basilica of St. Peter without a visit to Michelangelo's breathtaking Pietà, but I never enter without a pause at the Chair of Peter. Gian Lorenzo Bernini did artistically for the 17th century what Michelangelo did for the 15th and 16th, and one of his great works is the gilt bronze chair held aloft by SS. Augustine, Ambrose, Athanasius and John Chrysostom. The bronze chair was executed by Bernini at the request of Pope Alexander VII to encase a beautifully constructed wooden chair, believed for centuries to have been used by St. Peter himself, first pope of all. Such was the belief in 1666, when the wooden chair was placed inside the bronze chair as if in a huge reliquary.

The only problem, discovered by a couple of archaeologists two centuries later, and verified by studies requested by Pope Paul VI in the 20th century, is that St. Peter never sat in the highly prized wooden chair. It was apparently a throne that the monarch Charles the Bald caused to be made for himself in the ninth century. When Charles was crowned as Emperor in St. Peter's Basilica on Christmas Day in the year 875, he donated his throne-chair to the pope! The centuries created a legend. The chair of Charles the Bald became the chair of Peter, but only with a small "c."

And therein lies the important part of the story. The Feast of the Chair of St. Peter is not a feast in honor of a four-legged object, of whatever material, regardless of who ever sat in it. The "Chair" of Peter, or of any pope, is the symbol of his teaching authority. The technical term for this in Greek is *cathedra*. When we describe infallibility — freedom from error — we give as a condition that the pope must speak "*ex cathedra*," "from the chair," that is, in his official role as *the* teaching authority of the Church. In every cathedral we find a *cathedra*, a chair used only by the bishop. When speaking from the chair in his own cathedral, the bishop is speaking to the Church in his diocese as its official teacher.

On the Feast of the Chair of St. Peter, then, we celebrate the teaching authority of the first pope, given by Jesus Himself. "Simon, son of John . . . feed my lambs, feed my sheep." Simon, of course, was Peter; the name given him by Christ, Peter the rock, on which Christ would build His Church. It was to Peter that Jesus would say, "I have prayed for you, Peter, that your faith may not fail and when you have turned to me, you must strengthen the faith of your brothers." To Peter, first, He would give the keys of the kingdom of heaven.

But it was also to Peter that Jesus would say: "When you were young, you used to get ready and go anywhere you wanted to; but when you are old, you will stretch out your hands and someone else will tie you up and take you where you don't want to go." St. John tells us that Jesus was indicating the way Peter would die — by crucifixion — but when I read this passage I like to think of the frail elderly, as well, and the sick and the vulnerable: all those dependent on others with a dependency not always easy.

Of course, although the Chair of Peter is not really a chair, the remains of the body of Peter are, indeed, buried beneath the great basilica which was built precisely to house them. Our Lord's prophecy was verified. Peter was bound and crucified. His body was buried. His remains are in the basilica. But the Chair of Peter symbolizes the teaching authority of the man made a teacher by the Master, and the teaching authority of every single one of that man's successors, of whom John Paul II is the latest.

It's worth reflecting on this, especially during Lent. It won't necessarily make us any holier, but it's comforting to remember that we have a guide who goes back a long, long time.

Life Issues:
Right to Life, Euthanasia, Care of the Handicapped, etc.

The Joy of Teaching Mimi

I would like to tell you briefly about the little girl who stole my heart back in 1962. I had begun a First Holy Communion class for retarded children. We had quickly gone from the local conviction that "there are no retarded children around here" to about 20 youngsters, some with Down's syndrome, some with brain damage, some with other difficulties. Mimi would usually stay in her seat for about two minutes, then be up and running around the room, stamping her feet, screaming, banging anything that would make a noise. Routinely I would evict her. Routinely she would return, quietly, after all of a minute outside the classroom.

Mimi had never eaten a meal at her family's table, despite their overwhelming love and desperate desire to help. Her eating habits matched her classroom behavior — dishes slammed to the floor, food thrown at the ceiling.

You can never really make a long story short without leaving out almost everything important, but I have no choice. After six months I received a telephone call which thrills me as much in the recollection as in the event. It was Mimi's mother. She had called me many times. I knew immediately this time was different. "Father, you'll never guess." I suggested she try me. "Mimi ate dinner with us last night at the dining room table."

Anyone who ever spent so much as a half hour working with retarded children knows what that call meant. There is not a parent who has ever been gifted with a retarded child who wouldn't thrill with the parents of Mimi.

It's over 30 years since Mimi's mother called me. I wish I could say that everything has changed since then for families with retarded children.

Some wonderful research has been carried out, of course. Lots of new and exciting educational programs have been developed. Some superb institutions have come into being. But there is still so much public fear, so much public ignorance. There are still parents who feel guilty, who imagine God is punishing them for some long-ago sin. There are still those who are so very lonely, who don't know whether to keep their child at home or to turn to an institution; still those who refuse to believe that their child is, in fact, retarded. It's all still there today, so many years later.

And most of all what's still there, I'm afraid, is immense unawareness. It's not that people are indifferent; it's simply that they don't know. I regret to say, for example, that despite our special religious education activities throughout the archdiocese, despite the Astor Home and St. Agatha's and a host of other marvelous institutions in the archdiocese, many of us are unaware of the tremendous religious potential of the retarded. If we haven't worked with them, we are unaware of what Sister Anne Ryan calls their "intuition for the sacred."

The retarded seem instinctively to love God, once they have heard about Him at all. But if you have never taught a retarded child the meaning of the Sacred Body and the Precious Blood of Our Lord, you have missed an extraordinary joy. I can never be adequately grateful for that joy myself. I hope that everyone in or responsible for religious education in the Archdiocese of New York, especially in our parishes, will some day have — or make — the opportunity given me, to teach our retarded youngsters everything they are capable of learning about God and His Blessed Mother. You'll be astonished at how much that is.

Statistics Don't Tell the Human Tragedy

It was as stark a letter as I have seen:

A member of our family, age 27, mother of four small children, had been using heroin and pills for 11 years. They were years of continuous torment for her, which included prison, emergency rooms, detoxification, crime, running, etc.

Last week she got tired and seemed genuinely

sincere about cleaning up. She went to (name withheld) two times. Both times she was high and sent away. She was asked to come back on Monday morning, when she would be sent to a hospital to be detoxified and then possibly sent to a residential facility.

She did not show up for her appointment because she died of a heroin overdose today . . . Our hearts are shattered by this tragedy.

The letter was signed. The people are real.

I have all sorts of statistics in my files: the estimated annual imports of drugs in the United States, the number of drug abusers, drug abuse among students, estimated annual spending on illegal drugs, and on, and on, and on — all statistics. Not one of them tells me of hearts shattered by tragedy, of children without a mother, of a mother in torment, in emergency rooms, in prison, in detoxification, of a mother running.

Not one figure tells me of flesh and blood, and human dignity, and the sacredness of the human person made in the image and likeness of God. Not one figure, such as the $120 billion spent annually on illicit drugs, tells me about the contempt for the human person that threatens to turn our society into a jungle while fortunes are made.

Each year we continue to kill more than a million and a half children waiting to be born in their mothers' wombs. Not one is a statistic. Every one of them is a human being.

It all goes together and we can't see it — this contempt for human life. Fortunes are made on abortion. Billions and billions of dollars change hands.

I am a great believer in the concept attributed to my friend, Cardinal Bernardin: "consistent ethic of life." The only problem I see in it is that many people who pretend to believe in it really don't. They pick and choose, and virtually every issue *except* abortion is given priority. They see relationships between and among every evil in the world, except between such evils and the contempt for human life that marks the abortion industry.

I must be obsessed. I see what Mother Teresa sees in abortion and what she called it in her Nobel Prize acceptance speech — the greatest obstacle to peace in the world. I see the same contempt for human life in the illicit drug industry that I see in the abortion industry.

I am not speaking of condemning the woman or young girl who has been misled or confused into having an abortion any more than I am speaking of condemning the 27-year-old woman of the above letter who died of heroin. I am talking about the cruel business of contempt, the business that nets countless billions of dollars for both abortionists and drug purveyors. It's filthy money.

Far from condemning, we are trying to do everything we can in the Archdiocese of New York to help the victims of contempt. For those pregnant women or girls in need, who cannot take care of themselves, we repeat our offer. We are prepared to provide medical care, hospitalization, counseling, adoption services, free of charge. For those who have experienced the tragedy of abortion, we want to help you start life all over again. For those tempted to have an abortion, we want to provide you the alternative of life for your baby and for yourself.

We want very much, as well, to help both victims of drug abuse and those who are tempted. Our Office of Substance Abuse Ministry is available to all, as are a variety of programs for both prevention and rehabilitation.

We happen to believe unconditionally in the "consistent ethic of life," and we are trying to practice it.

Your Baby Is Precious

My beloved niece delivered a beautiful little baby girl on the day after Thanksgiving. The cost was quite high; some would call it excessively high. She had been hospitalized for almost three months before they could take the baby by Caesarean section.

Post-delivery complications developed and she came very close to death. A lot of surgical skill, blood transfusions and prayer brought her through. She believes the baby was worth every minute of it. So does her husband.

Who can count the number of young women willing to sacrifice, to suffer, to run extraordinary risks to bring babies into the world? They are legion. How many would do it for a "thing" — a piece of tissue, an unidentifiable blob of matter? They know — they know it's a *baby* they're fighting for and sacrificing and suffering for, and willing to give their own lives for.

Our baby (my niece's) is healthy and whole. We are deeply grateful. But for many years of my life as a priest I have worked, off and on, with the mentally retarded. I have taught them, prepared them to receive the sacraments, worked with their parents. The love that I have found in the homes of countless numbers of families blessed by a retarded child is indescribable. I know parents who are deeply bitter, desperately frustrated and I understand. But for every such parent, I know a dozen who are as grateful for their retarded child as my niece for her healthy little baby. They see the image of God, they see a profound impact on their family life, an impact that has strengthened them, and given them new insights, and led them to new-found family harmony, and taught them things about *themselves* they had never known before.

There's a booklet on my desk, a marvelous booklet called "Thanks be to God." It was written and illustrated by the mentally retarded and developmentally handicapped students of the Marian Center in Miami, a center conducted by the wonderful Sisters of St. Joseph Cottolengo, who are paralleled in our own Archdiocese by our Daughters of Charity and Cabrini Sisters and Blauvelt Dominicans and Franciscan Sisters and many others. I wish everyone could see this booklet. I wish particularly that it could be seen by those fearful of having a retarded or handicapped child, and by those who have not yet been able to accept such a child — those who feel guilty, or resentful, or bitter, or ashamed, and who ask "Why?" There are some 30 drawings in the booklet, in brilliant color. They all look pretty much like — "normal" children's' drawings in early grades, but well beyond the "stick figure" stage. What strikes me about them, however, is that every man, woman and child and every dog and cat in every drawing but one, has the mouth with the turned up corners that depicts happiness in every language. And remember, these aren't the drawings of adults showing retarded and handicapped youngsters as we would like them to feel. These are retarded and handicapped youngsters drawing the world as they see it.

Only one drawing shows sadness. It depicts the death of the founder of the Sisters of St. Joseph Cottolengo. The sisters are standing and kneeling by Joseph's bedside, praying their Rosaries, with their mouths turned down at the corners, with big oval tears literally falling to the ground from their eyes. Only Joseph's mouth is turned up in a great big smile, as though he knows precisely where he's going, and is delighted by the idea. "Out of the mouths of babes," Our Lord reminds us in the Gospel, "comes wisdom." Thanks be to God, says the happy little booklet.

My beloved niece almost died in having her beautiful little baby girl. I know a large part of myself would have died with her. I know, too, that she is blessed with a family of great faith and great love that not every pregnant woman has. She never for a moment dreamed of abortion. I can understand why many women would. That's why we plead with any pregnant woman so tempted, to come to us, to call 1-800-592-HELP, to be received with love and with care, to be given the help needed not otherwise available, be it medical, or financial, be it the need for a home, for hospitalization, for help in keeping a baby or in arranging for adoption. You may not be my niece, but you are exceedingly precious to God and to me. And so is your baby.

"Consistent Ethic of Death"

From the very outset I have agreed with my good friend Cardinal Bernardin's use of the term "consistent ethic of life." He has rightly insisted that every life is sacred, at every moment of its existence. To be consistent, if I am to be truly concerned about the unborn, because they are human beings, I cannot be indifferent to what lies ahead for them when they are born, or insensitive to the poor, the hungry, the homeless, the oppressed, the discriminated against. I cannot be callous about enormous arms expenditures or the ravages of guerrilla and counter-guerrilla warfare, or the threat of nuclear war. Human life is human life, and I must respect its sacredness at all times and in all circumstances.

The trouble has never been with Cardinal Bernardin's formula, nor with his own use of it, but with misuse and abuse by some whose attitudes toward abortion and the traditional pro-life movement leave a great deal to be desired. The "consistent ethic of life" principle was never intended to mean that every "life" issue is as important as every other "life" issue. It is unjust to pay a woman less than a man for doing the same job. A tax structure is unjust that makes the poor poorer. It is unjust to treat blacks or other "minorities" as second class citizens. It is outrageously unjust to pour dependent psychotics into the streets, to create massive homelessness for the poor through massive gentrification for the wealthier, to ignore the arms race, and the monstrous imbalance of standards of living between our world and the Third World or the Fourth.

All of these are life issues. They vary in importance, in urgency, in ways of bringing about solutions. There is nothing sacred about any given tax structure. One designed with the best intentions in the world may turn out to be a nightmare. Tax experts, economists and public officials may legitimately differ on what may work. They may not legitimately differ in the requirement to seek justice for all.

The same may be said for employment practices, treatment

of psychotics, the distribution of wealth, the best way to solve the housing shortage, what constitutes a just war, or a just means of waging war or of securing peace.

All these and many other issues are "life" issues. All differ in degree, in urgency and in "absoluteness" from the issue of the direct immediate unarguable killing that we call abortion. I get sick at heart over the street people, particularly in mid-winter. If I try hard enough, however, and care intensely enough, I can do *something* to at least lessen their suffering. For example, I can provide temporary shelters for many of them. That's far from being an adequate solution to an immensely complex problem, but it's *something*. I can do nothing for a dead baby. In millions of cases, I can't even bury it. There are not degrees in abortion. There are no shades of difference. Death is death.

If anti-abortionists seem compulsive "one issue" persons to some, it is often that they fear the one issue will be demeaned, diminished, deliberately downgraded when addressed as but one issue in a broad range of "life" issues about which we must be consistent.

I wonder if we could buttress Cardinal Bernardin's legitimate and useful "consistent ethic of life" approach by recognizing a parallel ethic that is as destructive as the "life" ethic is constructive. We might call it the *consistent ethic of death*.

We started the death march by legalizing abortion in highly restrictive circumstances, pretending that we were not killing unborn babies but that, even if we were, circumstances justified it. In no time at all, we had Supreme Court decisions that legalize killing unborn babies up to seconds before their birth. It didn't take long after such decisions for a Nobel Prize winner to argue that parents should have until at least three days after a birth to decide whether or not a "defective" baby should be allowed to continue living.

So the inexorably consistent ethic of death continues, with life at the other end of the spectrum from the unborn now under continued threat. "Death with dignity" has become the polite description for putting elderly people out of their misery, determining that the "quality of life" of the cancer patient has deteriorated to an unacceptable point, deciding that an individual can no longer live "productively." It's a fancy term — like "terminating pregnancy" and "pro-choice." *Living wills* are springing up all over the place.

How long will the death march continue to be voluntary? If the baby in a mother's womb is given no choice about being put to death, will the day come when the elderly, or the "prematurely senile" will be considered to be in their second childhood, and given no choice about being put to death?

I think there may be something to the term, "consistent ethic of death." It can certainly be applied to a broad spectrum of "death" issues, as the "consistent ethic of life" can be applied to a broad spectrum of "life" issues. Who knows? It might help change our viewpoints. We might get a view of death from the perspective of the unborn, the infant, the retarded, the wheel-chaired, the cancer-ridden, the aged — or even the starving, the freezing, the bagmen and bagladies struggling to survive the night.

Thank You, Mr. Nat Hentoff

Nat Hentoff calls himself a Jewish atheist libertarian, regardless of his wonderfully prophetic beard. Be that as it may, he wrote a two-part series on me in the *New Yorker* which was far more flattering than will be the eulogy that some poor priest or bishop will have to preach over me when I lie "in state," as we say, in the middle aisle of St. Patrick's Cathedral. Despite that temporary fall from grace, Mr. Hentoff has to be one of the best writers in the United States.

Naturally, I wish Mr. Hentoff always wrote things I agree with. He doesn't. But even when I think Nat Hentoff is dead wrong, I thank God he's such a gifted writer, and that he cares passionately about the issues he addresses. The passion and the

caring show up again in his *Village Voice* series on euthanasia,
brought to my attention by Dr. Joseph R. Stanton of The Value of
Life Committee, Inc., in Brighton, Mass. In a letter enclosing
copies of the Hentoff articles, Dr. Stanton told me I am "one of 30
people" to whom the mailing was being sent. I wish I were one of
30 million, including, most particularly, every doctor and every
lawyer, legislator and judge in the United States.

The *Village Voice* articles began on Aug. 25, 1987 under title
of "The American Death Squads." Speaking of an April 12, 1984,
article by 10 physicians from some of the most prestigious medical
schools in the U.S. and published in the awesome *New England
Journal of Medicine*, he tells us that these "healers" advocated the
withdrawal of feeding tubes and hydration, among other things,
"allowing the patient to die."

"The last five words are, of course," says Mr. Hentoff,
"classic newspeak. In situations like this — George Orwell could
have told the 10 doctors the patient is being killed." The highly
vaunted "right to die" that euthanasiasts have been selling us for
years under a multitude of slogans — the latest is "death with
dignity" — is actually, Mr. Hentoff notes, "the right to kill."
Introducing the case of Nancy Ellen Jobes who died in New Jersey
when deprived of food and hydration, he tells us:

> As we shall see, fewer doctors each year are fighting for
> certain patients' lives. Instead, they are helping the
> courts ease the removal of more barriers of killing.
> When Nancy Ellen Jobes died, the United Handicapped
> Federation — but not any medical association — pro-
> tested her having been starved to death. 'She was
> welcome in the disability rights community,' these
> mourners said.
>
> 'It is now a capital offense,' said an anti-euthana-
> sia group, 'to be young, brain-damaged' — and too
> tenacious to die.

Next in the Hentoff series is "The Death Doctors." Calling the advent of the *Hippocratic Oath* "a profound change in the consciousness of the medical profession" and "an extraordinary moment in the history of civilization," he quotes famed anthropologist Margaret Mead on the subject of the oath:

> 'For the first time in our tradition there was a complete separation between killing and curing . . . With the Greeks, the distinction was made clear. One profession . . . was to be dedicated completely to life under all circumstances, regardless of rank, age, or intellect — the life of a slave, the life of the Emperor, the life of a foreign man, the life of a defective child.'
>
> 'This is a priceless possession which we cannot afford to tarnish,' Mead emphasized, 'but society always is attempting to make the physician into a killer — to kill the defective child at birth, to leave the sleeping pills beside the bed of the cancer patient. . . . It is the duty of society to protect the physician from such requests.'

Mr. Hentoff quotes from the *Hippocratic Oath* itself:

> . . . I will use treatment to help the sick according to my ability and judgment, but never with a view to injury and wrongdoing. Neither will I administer a poison to anybody when asked to do so, nor will I suggest such a course. Similarly I will not give a woman a pessary to cause abortion. . .

How shocking, then, the decision by the council on ethical and judicial affairs of the American Medical Association calling it ethical for doctors to withhold food and water under specified circumstances.

This is radically different, note, from withholding or withdrawing extraordinary medical treatment hence, permitting a patient to die of a given disease or illness. When food and water are withheld or withdrawn, the patient dies, not of the disease, but of starvation and dehydration. Mr. Hentoff quotes Dr. Norman Levinsky, chief of medicine at Boston University Medical Center, as saying that the A.M.A. ruling "gives doctors and other caregivers a message that it's O.K. to kill the dying and get it over with."

Both of these Hentoff articles are frightening, neither more so, however, than the others in the series. "The Deadly Slippery Slope," Sept. 1, take us from Karen Ann Quinlan back in 1976, to Nancy Ellen Jobes in 1987, and concludes:

> This year, the New Jersey Supreme Court broke its promise not to authorize life-and-death decisions on the basis of an individual's 'quality of life.' It authorized the killing of Nancy Ellen Jobes because her 'quality of life' wasn't good enough.
>
> See how far we have come in only 11 years. And consider how many more people are not, some say, worth keeping alive.

"The Useless Eaters" and "Should Paul Brophy Have Been Put to Death?" (Sept. 15 and 22 respectively) reveal no less shocking stories.

If even one doctor, one legislator, one judge is persuaded to stop the killing, to reject the consistent ethic of death we are developing in the U.S. with horrifying speed, by reading these articles, I would be pleased.

I thank Mr. Nat Hentoff, self-styled Jewish atheist libertarian, for reminding us of the urgency of the cause. I wish a lot more Catholics were writing as passionately about life as he is.

A Matter of Life and Death

My belief in the tremendous potential of suffering was born long before I read Dostoyevsky. It began in early childhood, with the standard reply given by my mother and father to my complaints about a toothache, an earache or a rainstorm that ruined a long-anticipated day at the beach, a very rare day, indeed, in our family. "Offer it up!" God will use your pain and your disappointment for His own purposes.

I didn't understand, of course, at least clearly (although I have never regretted having parents who didn't believe I had to *understand* everything they told me, as long as I did it), but the advice stuck to my bones, grew with me as my bones grew, became flesh and blood of my deepest beliefs as an adult. I have said it before, I have preached it incessantly from an altar made of a board slung over two torpedoes in the after-torpedo room of a submerged submarine, from innumerable altars called hospital beds throughout the world, from the magnificent Renwick altar of St. Patrick's Cathedral: the power of suffering is incalculable. I consider the sick and dying of the Archdiocese of New York, those eaten by cancer, shattered by AIDS, convulsed by seizures, isolated by mental disorders, distorted by uncontrollable spasms — I consider them, with the retarded, the handicapped, the wheelchaired, the blind, the lonely, the abandoned, indescribably valuable resources of grace for the Church in New York and for all society.

I repeat what I have said so often: The salvation of the world was not made possible by Christ's teaching or preaching, by His miracles, by His vigor in going up and down the land, often without food, without sleep. The salvation of the world was made possible only by Christ's suffering and death on the Cross. Only when He appeared utterly helpless to the world, totally useless, quivering with agony — only then did He begin to exercise His power, only then did He enter into the fulfillment of His mission on earth. I don't understand it for a fraction of a moment, but it is categorically true.

Neither do I understand how it is that if I unite my sufferings with those of Christ on the Cross — my toothache, or headache, or heartache, my temptations, the guilt I feel over my sins — whatever my sorrow or whatever its cause — I help Christ continue the salvation of the world. I believe this with all my being.

Because I can validate my belief in the Sacred Scriptures and in Church teaching, I don't need Dostoyevsky to support my own convictions, but as one who has long considered Dostoyevsky far and away as one of the greatest writers he has ever read (despite his bitter hostility toward Roman Catholicism), I deeply appreciate his articulating the meaning of suffering so very powerfully in so many of his extraordinary works (his *Diary of a Writer*, *The Idiot*, *The Possessed*, *Crime and Punishment*, *The Brothers Karamazov*).

I quote briefly, for example, from his *Diary*, in which he speaks of the Russian people of whom he says:

> ... the principal school of Christianity from which they have graduated is ... those centuries of innumerable and interminable sufferings which they have endured in the course of their history, when, forsaken and oppressed by everybody, toiling for everybody, they remained with no one but Christ — the Consoler whom they then embraced forever in their soul, and who, as a reward for this, has saved their soul from despair!

For Dostoyevsky it was *only* through suffering that the Russian people received Christ, or that *anyone* can receive Christ.

Why am I writing again about a belief I have expressed so often before? For two reasons.

First, because I am always having my own faith in this belief renewed in people I meet, so that I become that much more committed to spreading the belief for others. Only a week or so ago I visited a man obviously dying of complications related to AIDS. "You don't know how I am suffering," he told me. "I cannot begin to tell you how horrible I feel." I talked with him about the sufferings of Christ, observed how Christ was spread out on the Cross, as he, the patient, was spread out on the bed, feeling helpless, suffering horribly, but saving the world. I asked the patient to join his sufferings to Christ's, and told him he could become the most powerful man in New York by so doing. I will never forget the look of wonder on his face, or his joy or his words of gratitude. So that's my first reason for writing once again about suffering.

My second reason might seem quite removed, but really is not. A frightening number of people are being condemned to death by the courts, at the request of loved ones or "proxies," or by their own personal request. The reason: they are suffering "needlessly"; their lives are "useless"; they are terminally ill, or comatose, or "have nothing to live for." What an enormous difference it could make to such patients or to those acting on their behalf, if they understood the power of suffering. What a difference their suffering could make to the world, if they "offered it up."

Easy to say, because I'm not one of them? No. I try to suffer with every sufferer, to absorb his or her agony, or loneliness or despair. I may not succeed, and I may, in fact, offer little comfort, but I still believe passionately in the objective reality of what I have preached for so long, and pray that I will practice it on my own death bed.

I am not suggesting for a moment, of course, that only those should be saved from "mercy killing" (or whatever other euphemistic term may be used for "pulling the plug") who can come to understand the potential value of their suffering. Whether they, or we, understand that value or the mystery beneath it is irrelevant to the basic truth that only God has ultimate power over life. That power cannot be arrogated by *any* human being, a doctor, a judge, a legislator, a patient, a proxy — *any* human being.

Ecclesiastes reminds us that there's a time for speech and a time for silence. The implication is that the prudent man chooses whichever he believes will be more effective. Everyone likes to win every battle he fights. I have been in the Pro-Life Movement too long, however, to settle for victory in a battle or two. I want to win the war.

In the meanwhile, those suffering unto death merit our thanking them for their testimony to life—and for helping us save our souls.

We Had Better Wake Up

I'm reading a book on Oliver Wendell Holmes that's not making me very happy. It's called *Honorable Justice*, written by Sheldon M. Novick, and it received good reviews, which it deserves.

So it's not the writing, it's the man Holmes, Justice of the Supreme Court from 1902 to 1935, that makes me unhappy. As a matter of fact, it's not even the man, I suppose — I'm sure he was a great man, in many ways. It's what I believe he did to the law, and through the law, to all society, that distresses me.

Our Declaration of Independence calls upon the Laws of Nature and of Nature's God. One after another of our Founding Fathers, including Justice James Wilson, appointed by President Washington, were steeped in the tradition of Natural Moral Law. So was Cicero, nearly two thousand years before them, so was St. Paul, as is clear in his letter to the Romans, and so were the philosophers of the Middle Ages, and those later philosophers in the days preceding our American Revolution, like John Locke. Our entire Constitutional Tradition was rooted in Natural Moral Law.

What was so important about Natural Moral Law? It offered us moral absolutes. As Cicero put it: "There is in fact a true law, right reason, which is in accordance with nature, applies to all men and is unchangeable and eternal . . . this law summons men to the performance of their duties, by its prohibitions it restrains them from doing wrong . . . it will not lay down one rule in Rome and another in Athens . . . but there will be one law eternal and unchangeable, binding at all times upon all peoples."

Justice Holmes rejected that concept and all absolutes in morality. He saw the law as rooted purely in what is expedient, particularly what is politically expedient. His thinking was revealed clearly in such decisions as those favoring sterilization of "mental defectives" — forerunner of the notion of "racial hygiene." I quote:

> We have seen more than once that the public welfare may call upon the best citizens for their lives. It would be strange if it could not call upon those who already sap the strength of the state for these lesser sacrifices, often not felt to be such by those concerned, in order to prevent our being swamped with incompetence. It is better for all the world, if instead of waiting to execute degenerate offspring for crime, or to let them starve for their imbecility, society can prevent those who are manifestly unfit from continuing their kind. The principle that sustains vaccination is broad enough to cover cutting the Fallopian tubes . . . Three generations of imbeciles are enough.

That's chilling. Why am I talking about it so many years later — simply because I'm reading a book? No; I have known of Justice Holmes' legal philosophy for a long time.

I write at this point because, in my view, the same kind of thinking that approved forced sterilization of "mental defectives" is behind the arguments we hear today about "quality of life." I believe we are on the verge of a horrifying change in our entire national tradition concerning the sacredness of all human life. The "euthanasiasts" are winning their legal battles promoting "mercy killing," the "right to die," and other euphemisms.

Dr. Leo Alexander was an official medical expert at the Nuremberg Trials of German physician-executioners of Nazi medical atrocities. He was horrified. As the editor of the prestigious *New England Journal of Medicine* put it: "The experience impelled him to record the insidious progression of corrosive medical thinking . . ." I quote from Dr. Alexander's report:

> Whatever proportions these crimes finally assumed, it became evident to all who investigated them that they had started from small beginnings. The beginnings at first were merely a subtle shift in emphasis in the basic attitude of physicians. It started with the acceptance of the attitude, basic in the euthanasia movement, that there is such a thing as life not worthy to be lived.

Dr. Alexander goes on to assert that this "entire trend of mind received its impetus" from "the non-rehabilitable sick."

As a nation, we had better wake up and care. We get caught up in all sorts of trivia and cosmetic legislation, while death stalks our elderly, our cancer-ridden, our handicapped, disabled, retarded, our vulnerable. Few people foresaw that permissive abortion legislation would result in the deaths of tens of millions of unborn babies since 1973. Even fewer seem to recognize — or to fear — the potential of the "pull-the-plug" court decisions taking place today and the permissive legislation that can be expected to follow. Who's next?

"I Saw Him That Day . . ."

I may be the only Archbishop of New York who had one lesson on the violin, and only one. Lessons cost a lot when I was 10 years old, as much as fifty cents an hour. The violin was free, and you took it home to practice. That was the problem.

My mother came into the bedroom and saw me practicing — flat on my back. I told her that was the way Rudolph Valentino had played the violin in "The Sheik." She told me I wasn't Rudolph

Valentino and more importantly "The Sheik" was a silent film, so it didn't matter if he played the violin standing on his head.

Fifty cents was fifty cents in those days. Back went the violin. I settled for joining the St. Clement's Cadet Drum and Bugle Corps, and learned to play both drum and bugle free — undoubtedly to get back at my mother.

That was a strange thing to be thinking about on a Saturday morning in St. Patrick's Cathedral as I listened to a young lad read during Mass for the Disabled. I had been told he had a severe learning disability, and that he had practiced incessantly for this monumental moment.

"Before God, who gives life to all things," he read, and every word was chisel-sharp, yet rounded and clear and from the bottom of his heart.

"How wondrous the love of those who teach him," I thought, "and the love of those who brought him into the world and who nurture him today."

That's when I remembered the violin and the drum and the bugle and a mother and father who loved me, and I marvelled at how much I have taken for granted over the years. I was able to walk and to talk at an average age, to see, to hear, to learn at an average rate, to read, throw a ball, catch a ball, beat a drum, blow a bugle, walk a dozen city blocks alone at the age of 10 to carry a violin back to its owner.

A wonderful couple came to see me recently. Their youngest boy, now 22, was an advanced learner, clever in mathematics, ebullient in temperament, cheerful, loving. Now he is in an institution. He is schizophrenic. The couple came to plead with me to "do something" to raise consciousness about "mental illness" as a very real and crushing disease. They have been blessed with the best doctors and the latest in medicines. Nothing has worked, but they want at least to help rid individuals and families of the stigma born of stereotyping and the pain that comes with our common usage of words like "crazy" or "nutty," or what will you.

They want to do far more about mental illness, of course, but they want at *least* respect for those afflicted.

I looked out at a sea of the wheel-chaired in the cathedral, that Saturday, and at a chorus of the deaf, at the young sightless woman who had read the second reading through her fingers, at the mothers and fathers and teachers of the brain-damaged, the retarded, the disabled who need round-the-clock care. What infinite respect they deserve, what gratitude from all society. They flood the world with their love, a world so steeped in gloom, so racked with contempt.

"I command you to obey your orders and keep them faithfully," the young reader read, "until the day when our Lord Jesus Christ will appear. His appearing will be brought about at the right time by God, the blessed and only Ruler, the King of kings and the Lord of lords. He alone is immortal; He lives in the light that no one can approach. No one has ever seen Him. To Him be honor and eternal power! Amen."

"Amen," I echoed to myself, and reflected that while I have never seen God face to face, which is what St. Paul's first letter to Timothy is talking about, I saw Him that day in the cathedral, in every one of those youngsters and oldsters, parents and teachers, blind, lame and halt; I saw Him and I was very glad.

And I felt infinitely grateful even to be able to tie my shoelaces.

The Sounds of Violence

Who in the world is listening to the sounds of violence? Really listening?

I worry sometimes that my mind seems to work differently from so many other minds, like the minds of many editors and columnists and sociologists and criminologists. I see connections that many legislators and judges and elected and appointed officials and television producers and movie script writers and various other shapers of our destiny do not seem to see at all.

I see, for example, the ethic behind a book such as Derek Humphry's best seller, *Final Exit*, as more explanatory of violence in our society than all the crack that has ever been sold and all the Saturday night specials ever loaded. *Final Exit* gets to the very bottom of violence: that there is such a thing as a human life without value. *Final Exit* is a do-it-yourself book about killing yourself or having yourself killed. It's a "how to" manual on suicide. It is but one piece in the end game of trying to legalize euthanasia, or "mercy killing," and "assisted suicide" in our nation. It is sweeping the country as efforts to stampede legislators to buy into the ethic of death are sweeping the country.

Is none of this related to the violence in our streets, our subways, our homes, our wars? Is none of this related to racism or anti-Semitism or hatred in a thousand other faces? Doesn't it all go together? If I consider *any* life not worth living, do I not ultimately devalue *every* life? Is contempt for human life ever really divisible?

Time after time when a widely publicized act of violence occurs, I am asked for a comment. I see eyes glaze over and boredom become palpable when I begin my reply, because it's the same every time; and that is, that no multiplying of police, no changes in the criminal justice system, no new social programs, however sophisticated and costly, will be effective until we recover a sense of the worth and dignity of every human person, the sacred human person, made in the Image of God.

Call my answer glib or pietistic. Call it an empty platitude or an evasion. It's the answer I will give until the day I die. Berate me for putting abortion and euthanasia on a continuum with every conceivable act of violence in between. Tell me there is categorically no relationship between street crime and legalized suicide. Call my connecting such outrages an obscenity, a sacrilege. But the sounds of violence have not been muted. They merely go, if not unheard, unnoticed, because they are but grace notes in the symphony of death that is replacing our national anthem.

A Human Judgment Call

After what seemed like the 23rd instant replay I turned off the television and went back to work. I was mad, not at the number of instant replays, but at the umpire. Anybody could see that Twins' first baseman Kent Hrbek pulled the Braves' Ron Gant off first base. Anybody but the umpire. He called Gant out. His was the only call that mattered. That's the way it should be whether I was fuming or not.

Baseball has become technical enough without using instant replays to overrule umpires. I'm told that some managers have computers that tell them how a right-handed designated hitter will probably perform in any given two-out, bases-loaded, left-handed-pitcher situation. That's not my kind of baseball. I prefer a human judgment call. It takes more courage; and sometimes more faith.

The lady that somebody had written to me about might not appreciate my having thought of her the other night after I turned off the ball game. Her situation, after all, was a matter of life and death, of courage beyond measure, and of a deep faith in a judgment beyond the story told by pictures.

But I did think of her, and I reread the letter about her with awe, no longer fuming over a ball game, no longer thinking of anything except a woman's courage and faith and a baby who will one day be a man among men thanks to that courage and faith.

After a brief explanatory opening the letter informed me of what the writer called a most wonderful "happening":

> A young lady who had served my school as a physical therapist became pregnant about 10 months ago. In her 16th week of pregnancy, a sonogram was performed and the doctors told her that no amniotic fluid appeared present and, therefore, her fetus would have no lungs or kidneys (Potter's syndrome). They suggested to her that she terminate this pregnancy since the fetus

would continue to grow within her womb, but once the child was born, it would not be able to breathe and, therefore, die immediately. She told the doctors that she was Roman Catholic and felt she could not do that and that she would continue the pregnancy. After that she had seven additional sonograms done, read by seven other doctors, all of whom told her the same prognosis, but she continued the pregnancy.

Three weeks ago, a baby boy, 3 pounds, 4 ounces, was born and immediately the doctor placed the child on her chest and told her to say a few words of good-bye to her son. Within minutes, the doctor then called for a pediatrician since the baby appeared to be breathing and normal. Although a premature weight, every indication is that the baby is normal and healthy. She, her husband, family, friends and I all attribute this miraculous birth to prayers. She is a religious young woman and told me that throughout her pregnancy she kept hearing the words, 'Walk by faith, not by sight,' and on the day following the birth of the child, she opened her Bible and found the quote in James. She was shocked and surprised at this revelation. I thought you might want to hear this story and perhaps share it with others.

My mind works unpredictably. An umpire's call reminded me of a letter. The letter reminded me of a fundamental principle: "First things first." The principle reminded me of the October 1991 issue of an extraordinary journal, *First Things*, edited by Richard John Neuhaus. A reading of the journal rewarded me with an article by John Sommerville, "Why the News Makes Us Dumb." The article quotes journalist Malcolm Muggeridge in a way that explains even more clearly why the lady of the letter looked beyond the sonograms.

"I've often thought," wrote Muggeridge, ". . . that if I'd been a journalist in the Holy Land at the time of our Lord's ministry, I should have spent my time looking into what was happening in Herod's court. I'd be wanting to sign up Salome for her exclusive memoirs, and finding out what Pilate was up to, and . . . I would have missed completely the most important event there ever was."

The Stuff Saints Are Made Of

Dear Cardinal O'Connor:
    . . . [The child] will be two years old this year. He came about not through an act of love, but as a result of fraternity date-rape at a "good" college. His mother, a lovely, bright, senior was so ashamed she denied to herself that she was pregnant. She did not confide her condition to anyone until three weeks before the child was born.
    Once she told her mother and me, we set about making the necessary medical arrangements.
    I was totally unprepared for the beauty, courage, wisdom and faith this young woman gave to us all.
    Along with her mother, I was present at the birth. We cried and laughed joyfully together as he was placed in her arms.
    Four days later she handed her son to another woman in front of a church, knowing she would never see him again but so firm in her love and conviction that she gave him to a family.
    No one knows, beyond her own family and my husband and me that she had a child. She has since graduated, is employed at a professional level and is a well-adjusted single woman. But not a day goes by that she does not think of her son and pray for him.

On Mother's Day, please do whatever you deem
appropriate in our Church liturgy, and in the media, to
recognize the sacrifices of these mothers, the mothers
who loved so much, the ones who had so much faith in
life as to bear a child and give it to another.

The letter is signed and bears an address. It is as authentic as
it is hauntingly beautiful.

I would add but a brief footnote. I would respect, as well,
those heroic mothers who keep their babies themselves, when it is
possible for them to do so and to do so is in the babies' best interest.
They should hold their heads high, those single parents. They, too,
have chosen life for the innocent, at whatever cost to themselves.

And that would be all I would add, except to thank the writer
for one of the most touching letters I have ever received; to thank
her and the others who helped save a young mother and her baby;
to thank the same young mother for her courage; to thank the
family who offered the new-born their home and their love; to
thank the countless numbers of unsung parents and others who
encourage a frightened girl or woman to let her baby live and see
her through every step of the way. You are the stuff that saints are
made of, all of you, and you do us proud. Thank God for you.

Would His 'Keepers' Have Believed Him?

The sudden frightening spate of news reports about aban-
doning aged and helpless fathers and mothers reminds me of the
week my mother drove my father out of his mind.

Even then it may not have been the right name, or the right
disease, and I don't know what they'd call it today, but I wasn't
surprised when they told me my father had "cerebral arteriosclerosis." His remote memory was spectacular — who married
whom, where, in what church, on which day in 1899 — that kind
of thing was on the tip of his tongue. But every once in a while he

would forget where he had been the day before yesterday. It was only once in a while, but frequently enough to deserve a name especially since he had become periodically subject to convulsions.

Whatever the cause, he seemed able to manage quite nicely by way of regular doses of a mysterious red liquid medicine, obligingly provided by the local pharmacist who knew both my father and a doctor my father had once consulted in a very dim and distant past — like maybe 10 years in the dim and distant past. The doctor had died. The medicine continued.

Then one day my father began to look funny, walk funny, talk funny, but in a way that didn't make us laugh. There was clearly something strange going on. It must be his cerebral arteriosclerosis! My mother had the answer immediately: double the red medicine. That's when my father threw his dinner plate at the ceiling. The catsup splattered its way becomingly over the walls. Within seconds, my father was sound asleep in his chair. He made the mistake of waking up an hour later.

"Tom," my mother called soothingly, as he looked around in bewilderment, "you must have forgotten to take your medicine for a few days. I'll make up for it."

Out came the red bottle from the cupboard above the refrigerator. Two more spoonsful dutifully poured down my father's unsuspecting throat. Back into a sound slumber, until the middle of the night, when *bang*! Out of bed. No! He's not going to throw that wooden chair at the ceiling. But he is. Oh, yes. He very much is. He had apparently developed something against ceilings.

We had to face it, and it was hard. My father had lost his mind. He could be dangerous. Send for a doctor, a psychiatrist. Get him to a neurologist. Do *something*!

I did. I took my father to a noted psychiatrist. He stared at my father. My father stared at him. He told me we had no choice but to lock my father up in a "mental ward." I had worked in those wards — those *back* wards as we called them in those days — where men screamed incessantly, or sat all day in filth, staring at the walls. Yes, we would do *something*; I didn't know what, but it would not be to lock my father in a ward.

I took him home. My mother gave him red medicine. I moved into the house, and tried to sleep on a couch on the first floor. I was on hospital duty at the time, so I would be dead tired when I would fall onto the couch at night. But I had rigged an electrified mat beneath the rug in my father's bedroom, so that if he should get up at night a bell would ring beside my couch when he stepped on the floor. I would be up like a shot, maybe 10 times in a night, then go off to the hospital early in the morning to make my rounds.

Days tumbled into weeks. I became punchier than my father, but my problem was readily diagnosable. Nobody could tell us what was wrong with him. The cerebral arteriosclerosis diagnosis had worn threadbare. We didn't believe it any longer. And in the meanwhile, my poor father would go from being a thousand miles from nowhere into a sudden fit of rage that would shake the roof off the house and my mother's hair off her head.

Were we frantic! And did we pray! Between giving my father triple and quadruple doses of red medicine, of course, and with increasing frequency.

Then came an archangel of a doctor, a neuro-psychiatrist brother of a priest friend. He had heard of our problem and had come to see for himself. He took one look at my father and asked me the question absolutely no one else had asked: "Is your father on any medication?"

"Yes," I told him, feeling utterly stupid in knowing he would ask me what it was and I would only be able to say, "red stuff." He did and I did. "Can I see it?" I went to the cupboard and brought it to him. He took one sniff.

"Your father is saner than you are," he said without ceremony. "You're poisoning him. He has bromide poisoning from this medicine. The more you give him, the worse he has to get." The humiliation couldn't begin to equal the relief. "Can you help him, Doctor?"

"Of course, I can help him. There's nothing wrong with his mind but this medicine. Throw it away and see that he never gets another drop of it. Then I'll give him something that will clean the bromide out of his system. After that, I'll give him a prescription that will take care of his original problem. But never, never again give him any kind of bromide."

My poor mother. I think she believed she would be in jail before daybreak.

That was 40 years ago. It was summertime. My father lived another 16 years, with never another convulsion. When he died at 86, his memory was shockingly better than mine is at this very moment. Indeed, he complained not infrequently that he remembered too many things he would have preferred to forget.

I often wonder what would have happened had we signed my father into a locked ward. Would the bromide poisoning have eventually worked its way out of his system? Would his "keepers" have believed him, then, when he would have insisted he was as sane as they were? Chilling to think of, isn't it? Very chilling to think of.

"No More Than the Life of a Louse . . ."

For years I have watched disbelief appear on peoples' faces as I have told them of Nobel Prize winners who have proposed a right to infanticide, the killing of infants. Drs. James D. Watson and Francis H. Crick, both Nobel Prize winners as co-discoverers of the double helix of DNA, each has had his say on the subject. Neither "say" is very pretty.

Dr. Watson is quoted as saying, for example: "If a child were not declared alive until three days after birth, then all parents could be allowed the choice that only a few are given under the present system. The doctor could allow the child to die if the parents so chose and save a lot of misery and suffering."

Dr. Crick is quoted somewhat differently but just as chillingly: ". . . no newborn infant should be declared human until it has passed certain tests regarding its genetic endowment and . . . if it fails these tests it forfeits the right to live."

As I said, people thought I was joking. Now come the Dutch doctors. I quote from a recent Associated Press story:

> An upcoming report proposing official guidelines for the mercy killing of severely handicapped newborns threatens to reignite the Dutch debate over euthanasia.
>
> The report by a committee of the Dutch Pediatric Association aims to expose a side of the euthanasia issue that until now has been kept in the shadows.
>
> After decades of official waffling despite public acceptance of euthanasia-on-request for adults, Parliament recently sanctioned guidelines that would grant immunity to physicians involved. . .
>
> [Dr. Zier Versluys, head of the association's Working Group on Neonatal Ethics] maintains euthanasia is part of good medical practice in neonatology, the treatment of the new-born.

Is this move toward "infant euthanasia" far removed, however, from what the U.S. Supreme Court already allows — that an unborn infant can be put to death seconds before birth? Does it differ much from the existing law in the state of Colorado? Advocates of human life in Colorado are now at work to bring about banning of second and third trimester abortions, and will consider it a great victory if they succeed.

You've probably heard of the proposed Freedom of Choice Act that our elected representatives in Congress are being pressured to pass. Its proponents don't try to conceal what it says, any more than Dr. Watson, or Dr. Crick, or the Dutch physicians, if all are accurately quoted. So, Congressman Don Edwards, House sponsor of the Act, says, "It provides for no exceptions — no exceptions whatever . . . a state may not restrict the right of a woman to terminate a pregnancy — *and that is for any reason."*

I truly believe we are developing a culture of death; indeed, we are far down the road. The Kevorkian suicide machine is but a symbol, and while its use gets headlines, much subtler signs of our national direction go unnoticed. The medical director of one of our finest medical centers told me recently that a major insurance agency, on which the very survival of the medical center depends, has warned him that he is keeping patients alive too long. If he continues to do so, the insurance agency could withdraw. These are *conscious* patients, not those in "irreversible" comas, who are relatively pain-free because of modern medications.

If the conscious, pain-free are at risk of being put to death, what of those who are allegedly in what is now popularly, but cruelly, being called a "permanent vegetative state"? What of those in acute pain, whom the euthanasiasts would "put out of their misery"? What of those who are a tremendous drain on family resources, financial or emotional? What of those who are just too much trouble to care for?

I turn sadly once again to a famous murderer, once only fictional, who I truly fear is now threatening to prowl our land in the flesh. His name is Raskolnikov, the main character of Dostoyevsky's *Crime and Punishment*:

> There are certain persons who have the right to commit breaches of morality and crimes. All men are divided into ordinary and extraordinary. Ordinary men have to live in submission, have no right to transgress the law because, don't you see, they are ordinary. But extraordinary men have a right to commit any crime and to transgress the law in any way just because they are extraordinary.

He continues to talk about the woman he had killed in order to steal her money:

A hundred thousand good deeds could be done and helped on that old woman's money which will be buried in a monastery. Hundreds, thousands perhaps, might be set on the right path. Dozens of families saved from destitution, from ruin, from vice, and all with her money. Kill her, take her money and with the help of it devote one's self to the service of humanity and the good of all. What do you think? Would not one tiny crime be wiped out by thousands of good deeds? For one life thousands would be saved from corruption and decay. One death and a hundred lives in exchange. It's simple arithmetic. Besides, what value has the life of that sickly, stupid, ill-natured old woman in a balance of existence? No more than the life of a louse, of a black beetle, less, in fact, because the old woman is doing harm wearing out the lives of others.

We'd *better* believe it!

Racism, Anti-Semitism, Social Problems, AIDS

"I Cannot Give Stones . . ."

It was the worst dream I ever had. There was a terrible famine. I was the only one who knew where there was a huge hollow mountain filled with bread. I told somebody that if he could get me a big helicopter, I would go to the mountain, fill the helicopter with bread, fly around dropping it to the hungry people, go back and fill it up again, and keep doing the same thing. The somebody got me a helicopter. I flew it myself to save room for bread. I almost hit the Empire State Building, but somebody moved it out of the way just in time.

I started toward the mountain, flying very low so I could call out to the people and tell them I would be back with the bread. They looked as if they didn't believe me, and I told myself it was because they had been starving for a long time and too many people had promised them bread and had never come back.

It seems to me that it was around Yonkers, because I believe I passed the gold dome of the seminary — but you know how dreams are — where I saw what looked like millions and millions of little round loaves of bread, gleaming in the sunlight. I circled a few times. Yes, that's what they were. "Wonderful," I said to myself, "exactly what the people need, and so much closer. Why should I fly to the mountain for bread?" Down I went.

I landed and was shocked to see that what looked like little round loaves of bread from a distance were really shiny, round white stones. Great. Much better for the people. They'll appreciate them a lot more.

They can look at them in the sunlight, throw them around, play games with them, even pretend they're bread. I piled so many stones in my helicopter I could hardly take off. In only a few moments I saw a crowd of starving people looking up to me and crying: "Give us bread!" I threw them some stones and woke up, freezing and shivering and feeling more depressed than I had ever felt in my life.

The dream is by no means the reason, or even the smallest

part of the reason, why I have virtually an obsession about my responsibility for teaching and preaching the truths of our Catholic faith. But every once in a while, when I reflect on the deep hunger for such teaching that characterizes our day, the dream comes flashing through my mind as though it were only last night I had gone through it.

I read a piece in the newspaper that tells me of a survey on the question of removing even food and water from certain terminally ill patients. The article tells me that 73 percent of the people surveyed approved removal. This encourages the medical profession, the article says, because it shows that they have popular support for their own convictions. Not what's right or what's wrong, but how many vote for it. It's the approach to contraception, to abortion, to extra-marital sex, to Mass on Sundays, to confession, to drugs, to the divinity of Jesus, to the teaching of the Church on *any* subject. Not what's right or wrong, what the Church teaches or doesn't teach, but how many vote for it.

I read such and I'm saddened. Yet I must ask myself honestly: "How are people to know? Who is teaching them? Where? When?" At most, 25 percent of our youngsters go to Catholic schools. Only a small percentage of the others go to comprehensive religious education programs outside school on a regular basis, through high school. A huge number of adults in our archdiocese have had minimal Catholic schooling. The average youngster has watched 20,000 hours of television, or 30 hours per week, by the time of graduation from high school, and has seen 16,000 televised murders. Much else of what is seen on TV is indescribable. The damage to family life, the perverted notions given about love, sex and marriage are incalculable.

Where is the average Catholic exposed to the opposite, to the positive, constructive teachings of our faith? Few, very few, do adult Catholic instructional reading, or take adult Catholic educational courses. This means that the average Catholic's formal instruction in our faith is received at Mass on Sunday, with the homily the primary mode of instruction.

I consider no responsibility as Archbishop of New York more serious than that of seeing that all our people, young and old, are given bread, not stones. I cannot give stones to people who are hungry for bread. The hunger that truly exists is far more widespread and critical in reality than in the worst dream I ever had. I know our priests and teachers and a great number of our parents are as serious as I am about satisfying that hunger with the bread of truth that we call our Catholic faith, the whole of that faith, the totality of truth. I have a dream that they'll succeed. Thank God it's a much more powerful dream than the dream I had of my own failure.

"The World Will Hate You"

Life is never easy; right now "Catholic bashing" seems to be the *in* thing. That gives me a degree of comfort. It suggests we must be doing some things right. Our Lord made it very clear: "Because you are not of the world, but I have taken you out of the world, the world will hate you . . . as it hated Me before you."

The Roman historian Tacitus lived through the early days of Christianity (56 A.D.-117 A.D.). He saw Christians come to Rome and Rome worried by their presence. They were countercultural, like the Church today. Tacitus wrote a book called *The Annals of Imperial Rome,* in which he described the burning of Rome during the reign of Nero, who ruled from 54-68 A.D. Here's Tacitus:

> . . . neither human resources, nor imperial munificence, nor appeasement of the gods, eliminated sinister suspicions that the fire had been instigated. To suppress this rumor, Nero fabricated scapegoats — and punished with every refinement the notoriously depraved Christians (as they were popularly called). Their originator,

Christ, had been executed in Tiberius' reign by the governor of Judea, Pontius Pilate. But in spite of this temporary setback the deadly superstition had broken out afresh, not only in Judea (where the mischief started) but even in Rome. All degraded and shameful practices collect and flourish in the capital.

Blaming the victim is an ancient, dishonorable and convenient practice. Neither the Church at large nor individual Christians should be the slightest bit surprised to hear from those who speak for this world's values that we are the ones who create problems, "stir up the people," impose our values on others whenever we proclaim, "This is what we believe." Remember the charge levied against Jesus standing before Pilate: "He stirs up the people."

Expect that, each of you who would be called "Christian." Expect it when you object to your school boards about the imposition of the world's values on children. Expect it when you object to your television stations about imposing the world's values about marriage and family life, and when you object to theater owners who show the movies they show, and to producers who produce them.

Expect it when columnists and editors who are censored for ethnic slurs or attacks on virtually any other people can romp all over the place at the expense of Catholics who dare to publicly uphold their faith, without a murmur from publishers or owners.

Expect to stand before the Pilates of the world each day of your life, my Christian brothers and sisters or any other good and decent people of other religious persuasions, and have the world wash its hands of you before it sentences you to death.

If you're going to be a real Catholic, expect to be treated like one and be glad, even if it doesn't make you *feel* good. Neither Christ nor the Church ever said that "feeling good" is the purpose of life. "If you would follow Me, take up your Cross." Not in all of history has Easter Sunday come before Good Friday.

The Shameful Question

I have always been grateful for what the Brooklyn Dodgers' Jackie Robinson did for baseball and for the country. The stereotype he had to destroy was absolutely frightening. It couldn't be spelled out more bluntly than in the conversation attributed to Brooklyn Dodgers' President Branch Rickey and Clay Hopper, manager of the Montreal Dodgers, where Jackie Robinson was being groomed for the big leagues.

The story goes that Jackie had just made a spectacular play. Rickey turned to Hopper with the words: "No other human being could have made that play." Hopper's reply was tragic: "Mr. Rickey, do you really think he is a human being?"

That was little more than 45 years ago, shortly before Jackie Robinson "broke the color line" and went up with Brooklyn in 1947. To his credit, that same year Mr. Hopper went to Mr. Rickey, and said: "You don't have to worry about that man. He's the greatest competitor I ever saw. And what's more, he's a gentleman."

From actually questioning whether Jackie was human to calling him a gentleman is a giant leap. But it was a leap made only after Jackie Robinson had proved himself — *proved* himself in a way never required of a white man. Whether a drunk, drug-pusher, wife-beater, thief, murderer, thug — no white man ever has to prove he is human. I tremble in having to ask if even today we take every black man or woman at face value as a human person, yet "Black History" is very largely the history of human persons having to prove they are human.

I suspect that some people tire when in response to almost every question asked me about problems in the world, from homelessness to crack to abortion to child abuse to whatever, my answer always begins in precisely the same way: "We can solve nothing until we come to believe passionately in the worth and dignity and sacredness of every human person as made in the Image of God." I wish Jackie Robinson were around today so we could ask whether he would agree.

The testing of Mr. Robinson didn't end in Montreal. When he came to Brooklyn he was told clearly that he was not to act like a ballplayer. He was to be quiet and docile, to take pitches thrown at his head without a murmur, never to argue with an umpire, never to reply to taunts from opposing players or fans. In other words, he had to prove he was more than some kind of extraordinarily skilled and powerful subhuman something-or-other.

In my opinion, what is so remarkable about Jackie Robinson's becoming as great an all-around ballplayer as the majors have ever seen is that for his first few years he had to play with "one arm," in that he had to restrain that passion which helps so much to make a ballplayer a ballplayer. He came close to a nervous breakdown for having to conceal his emotions.

Then he cut loose. He knew the game wasn't worth the candle if be couldn't be himself — which for a black of his day was another way of saying it wasn't worth having to prove he was a human being.

I said above that I was grateful for what Jackie Robinson did for the country. Without our ever consciously articulating it, he forced us to face *the* basic question — the shameful question — about black athletes. How very sad that many of us who call ourselves Catholics had to be called to face the same question about blacks.

My greatest fear is that the question still lurks in too many "Catholic" minds, disguised by a thousand euphemisms. Until it's rooted out once and for all, much of our preaching is "sounding brass and tinkling cymbals."

The Mystery of Evil

There are different kinds of madness. What kind would drive a knife into the Rev. Al Sharpton? The same kind that drove a bullet into the Rev. Dr. Martin Luther King Jr.? Who can know? Argue all you want about similarities or dissimilarities between the two men. They're not the issue. They can merely satisfy the consciences of those who want to evade the issue. One fact only is absolutely indisputable, whether we want to face it or not. Both men are black. That fact should force us to confront a reality even beyond madness, a reality that is, in a sense, the foundation of madness.

In theology we speak of the mystery of evil. As mystery, it is unfathomable. Philosophers and theologians have puzzled over it for centuries. If God is good and God created the world, how can there be so much evil in the world? There are no top-of-the-mind, quick and easy answers. Even the most profound answers — and there are a variety of them — leave the questioner unsatisfied.

Whatever perplexities confront theological speculation about the mystery of evil, however, the most frightening aspect of the evil of the human condition, from my viewpoint, is crystal clear — and monstrous. In the stories of mythology, and throughout the pages of history itself, in epoch after epoch, we read the tale and the suffering it conveys: the tale of man's "envy" of God. However anyone interprets the Adam and Eve story, it is the quintessential tale of such envy. "Why has God forbidden you to eat the fruit of the tree in the center of the Garden of Paradise? Because it is the tree of the knowledge of good and evil. Eat it and you will become like God. You will determine what is good, what is evil, what is right, what is wrong. You will determine it for yourself. No God will be able to tell you what to do, because you will have become God yourself."

The Nazi dream of "purifying" the human race was essentially a dream of replacing a God who had failed — had blundered into creating a virtually endless number of the imperfect, the defective, the non pure-blooded, white, blond Aryan, the less-than-superman. Only the Nazis would determine who was fit to live, who would die. Only the Nazis would determine what was good, what was evil. They would replace God by becoming gods. They could then justify every horror, every form of violence, in order to recreate the world in their own image and likeness — for the world's own good.

Perhaps no one ever spelled out where this inversion of morals would lead better than Fyodor Dostoyevsky, in his *Crime and Punishment*. Raskolnikov brutally murders a helpless old lady in order to steal the treasures she has hidden in her room. But he can kill her only after he convinces himself of two things: one, that she is vermin — less than human; two, that he can do a great deal for the world if her wealth becomes his. He muses on the morality of it all, and determines that it's up to him to decide what is good, what is evil. He becomes God.

The Rev. Dr. Martin Luther King Jr. was killed because he was "less than human," and his death would be good for the world. Whoever made that decision had become God, had determined what is good, what is evil, had decided to recreate the world without the likes of Dr. King and his followers.

With a trial undoubtedly forthcoming in the case of the attack on the Rev. Al Sharpton, no one wants to attribute a specific motive to an accused in advance. That's for judge and jury. What's for the rest of us is to recognize and confront what breeds such violence. Whatever the attacker or attackers intended to do, the act itself was of a piece with all such efforts to remake the world. If the intention was to kill the Rev. Sharpton, it was very probably rooted in the belief that the world would be better off without him "and his kind." That's to decide what's good, what's evil. That's to be God.

The great and tragic irony, however, is that the true God never solves problems with violence. He is a God of Peace. He never "saves" the world with hatred; only with love.

I write on the birthday of the Rev. Dr. Martin Luther King Jr., January 1991, while the Rev. Al Sharpton remains hospitalized and the world holds its breath in fear of the first shattering shot in the Middle East that will once again destroy what passes for peace in this broken world. [The Gulf War began on January 17, 1991.] It is not a day for men to become gods.

"Only 2.5 Million Black Catholics in the U.S."

A couple of papers made a stab at it, which is better than they did in 1987, as far as I can recall, but I read nothing in the secular press that even remotely suggested the importance of the National Black Catholic Congress held in New Orleans from July 9 to 12 in 1992.

A remark by Sister Jamie Phelps, O.P., Ph.D., in an address to some 85 bishops at the Congress revealed part of the reason why neither the media nor the country at large would take the Congress very seriously. She noted how casually we tend to say that we have "only" 2.5 million black Catholics in the United States. In other words, the fractional number of blacks who are Catholic hardly merits *anyone's* serious attention.

Sister Jamie is black. She teaches at Chicago Theological Union. She is an astute analyst of our culture. Her remark about numbers as an index of importance — or unimportance — was but one of several insightful points she made, but it hit me harder than did any other. The first image that jumped to my mind was of someone shrugging off the Apostles some 19 centuries ago because there were only 12 of them. Then I thought of the cynical question attributed to Joseph Stalin: "How many legions does the pope have?"

In other words, we of the Church could wring our hands over having so few Catholics among the 32 million blacks in the United States, or we could say, much more constructively, in my judgment: "What a treasure, what a powerhouse for good; what an example of dynamic faith we have in two-and-a-half million black Catholics!"

What a model we find in our black Catholics. How many of them have had to face conditions in our society that most of us never have had to endure. How many have had to struggle for economic survival, for social acceptance, for equal opportunity in education, in jobs, in housing, in you-name-it. How many of them, let's be painfully honest, have had to fight for, long for, plead for recognition in the Church itself. Archbishop John Francis Rummel of New Orleans, the very city in which the Black Catholic Congress was held, is dead less than three decades. Can we be proud of the fact that many of his own clergy and laity bitterly opposed him when he decreed that blacks would no longer be required to receive Holy Communion after whites? When he ordered the integration of all parochial schools in 1956, many Catholics appealed to Rome against him. Rome supported him, but even then integration was delayed until 1962. And how painful it is to recall that parishioners of a certain parish refused so adamantly to accept a black priest that Archbishop Rummel had to close the church. Is it less than a miracle that we have two-and-a-half million black Catholics?

For me, the excitement of the Black Catholic Congress was in recognizing that the 3,500 black Catholic participants represented so many hundreds of thousands as passionately committed to the Church as they are — and as knowledgeable and resolute. They are categorically on the move. They are determined to play an increasingly vital role in the Church and in society. What was crystal clear to me at the Congress was that the 3,500 black participants representing two-and-a-half million black Catholics were and are dead serious about the values without which our nation simply cannot survive: decency, dignity, human life, justice, responsibility, accountability, moral, spiritual and religious virtue. Would that every office holder and political candidate could have seen and listened to what the delegates to the Congress were saying.

Other duties precluded my remaining at the Congress for more than an evening and a day, but I heard some of the most intelligent, articulate and professional speakers that I have ever heard at any major gathering, whoever the participants, whatever the purpose. One Ph.D. outdid another in his or her analysis of our culture and in offering more rational solutions to national problems than I have heard in several hundred political speeches or read in the most sophisticated journals.

Were I a politician, I would think more than twice about the dominant theme of the Black Congress, *The African American Family*, and the thoughtfulness with which that theme was examined. And I would gamble that, while "only" two-and-a-half million blacks are Catholic, they represent far more of the thinking and values of the 32 million blacks in this country than many people bother to observe. For they are the values which make it possible for all of us to live as truly human beings, whatever our color.

I was proud to have some of our New York black Catholic delegates at the Congress pin over my shoulder the colorful African "kenta" unique to the New York delegation. I brought it home with me as a reminder that the New York delegates owe me something. They owe me their best thinking on the best recommendations coming out of the Congress. And the kenta will remind me as well of what I owe them and all our black Catholics: to work side by side with them to try to turn those recommendations into reality. Neither they nor I can do that without the support of the entire Church of New York.

In the Cathedral Crypt, a Prayer for Haiti

It's time to take Pierre Toussaint seriously. The situation in Haiti is a mess. The relationship between Haiti and the United States is a mess. The potential for massive violence is horrifying.

Meanwhile, the skeleton of a man of peace lies beneath the high altar of St. Patrick's Cathedral. I pass his crypt each morning as I enter the sanctuary to offer the 7:30 Mass. These days I pray for his intercession for the land where he was born into slavery, the land that has known little but oppression, starvation, occupation, terrorism, and war, for generation after generation. The dominant, often the only, hope of the poor has been by way of their parish churches, their Masses, the efforts of their priests and bishops and religious sisters and brothers and others who care enough about them to teach them to read and write, to know and to love God, to try to be happy, in a way the world knows little about.

Although the cause for the canonization of Pierre Toussaint has its cadre of supporters, and has been accepted in Rome, I wish I saw more popular enthusiasm and excitement right here in New York over the possibility of his being declared a saint. Why does interest seem modest, at best? Because he accepted his slavery when he might have fled? Because, when brought to New York, he supported his "owners" when they suffered financial reverses, nursed them when they were dying, delayed his own marriage to carry out what he believed to be his responsibilities toward them, even after they declared him free? Who can pretend to understand the mystery of love?

And love he did. Becoming wealthy by the standards of the day, even when technically in bondage, he tramped the streets constantly to feed the hungry, and spent himself night after night to visit the sick. Every day for 60 years he trudged to Mass in old St. Patrick's Church, passed by wealthy Catholics in their carriages who refused to pick him up because he was black, however bitter the weather. Time after time he was insulted, was refused a seat in the church he had rebuilt after a fire. Yet he went on, doing good, doing endless good.

Yellow fever was common to New York of the day. Whenever it struck, those who could leave left home in panic. Not Pierre. He would search fearlessly through the quarantined areas, seeking in house after house for the abandoned, taking the sick into his own home to nurse them.

Legions of slaves purchased their freedom with funds given them by this man who felt so free interiorly that he seemed indifferent to his own state of technical bondage. Children, black and white, received an education they could not have dreamed of except for the generosity of Toussaint. Those orphaned by successive plagues found a home built for them by Pierre.

Was this an Uncle Tom, to be scorned by those who believe

he should have been a militant activist against slavery? What nonsense. If ever a man was truly free, it was Pierre Toussaint. He respected activists. He did not believe their way should be his way, and if ever a man did things his way, it was Pierre Toussaint. If ever a man was a saint, in my judgment, it was Pierre Toussaint.

It is not Pierre Toussaint the slave or the freed man whose help I ask for Haiti as I pass his remains each morning, but the Pierre Toussaint who seems to me to have been as saintly a saint as the Church has ever canonized, albeit he still awaits the formal title that I cannot convey on him. Validation of a miracle is still being sought, and conditions in Haiti have not made the search easy. But no one can read this man's life — and the records are thoroughly authentic — without being awed by his holiness.

What has really worked in Haiti? Who really knows what will work now? With hundreds of thousands of lives at stake, the great powers of the world seem paralyzed. I watch the debates on television. I listen to equally sincere members of Congress share mutually exclusive ideas about what action should be taken. I respect both their intentions and the complexity of their task. But meanwhile, the remains of a man of peace lie serenely in a crypt beneath the altar of sacrifice in the Cathedral of St. Patrick. If his soul is where I believe it must be, he's a "natural" for those sincerely looking for peace in Haiti, the perfect mediator. He won't even mind not being visited in the crypt. He's too humble for that, and this is not a sales pitch to create a popular shrine. He can hear a prayer from any distance, especially the cry of the poor.

The Bits of Dreadful Trivia

It's almost at the very end of her diary, but I can't find the book on my shelf tonight, so I can only give the sense of it, without the poignant elegance of her own words.

Month after frightening month she had been hidden in the tiny apartment with her family and others, holding her breath with theirs every time the Gestapo searched the area. Threatened every day with discovery and certain sentencing to a concentration camp or to death or to both, by every psychological rule imaginable she should have been impossibly warped, a hopeless emotional cripple. She wasn't at all.

That's part of the reason why, of the entire beautiful *Diary of Ann Frank*, the words she scribbled so shortly before her hiding place was discovered and she died in the middle of her teens have intrigued me most, since I first read them many years ago. "I twist my heart inside out and upside down," she wrote, in essence, "and I think of what a fine person I could be, if there were no other people in the world."

The "no other people" she's talking about are not the dreaded police, but her own family and associates in their shared hiding place. It's the little things they say and do, the way they look and snore and make noise when they eat the food smuggled in to them. It's their correcting her and criticizing her manners, her hairdo, her daydreaming, her adolescent moods. *That's* what got to her, that and the scores of other bits and pieces of dreadful trivia inescapable even in a life wherein every knock on the door is a possible invitation to death.

It seems to me that such is what gets to most of us, however hard we try each day to manage the very ordinary demands of life. I do not ride the subways so often as I should, but my guess is that many who ride them every day, like most of the people I work with, find them utterly draining. It's not merely that they are too often hot and dirty, or break down too frequently, but that they are usually packed with people, too many of them angry and irritable, ready to explode if the train lurches, if they are accidentally bumped, if a foot is unintentionally stepped on. When there are very few people, the emotional strain can be equally severe. Does one of them have a knife, a gun? Is one of them on drugs? Will I get to work alive? Home alive?

One of the most extraordinary women I have ever known lived in a wheelchair, severely paralyzed. Her mother was what we used to call prematurely senile. Maybe today we would have a fancier name. I used to visit the two of them, and come away awed and exhausted. The mother's memory had long since eluded her. Every two or three minutes she would ask her wheelchaired daughter the time, or when they would be eating, or if the newspaper had arrived, or what the weather was like. Tiny things, trivial things, surely too meaningless to upset anyone. Of course not — not if asked once or twice a day. Try answering with a smile the same questions asked fifty times a day, a hundred times.

"We have already eaten, Mother." "It's three o'clock, Mother." "You have already read the paper, Mother."

Never a quiver in the younger woman's voice. Never a note of exasperation, a suppressed scream, a stifled sob.

And this day after day, month after month, year after year (some 10 years at the time I knew them).

The spiritual writers speak of "heroic sanctity." I have met it frequently, and almost inevitably it's in those who absorb the crushingly demanding trivia of life in a way that leaves me in awe.

I think that's what most filled me with awe in my recent 24 hours in Lourdes. It was not even the extraordinary sacrifices of those who had brought their loved ones, "hopelessly" ill, from hidden recesses of the world. It was their simple willingness to live among people, taxing, demanding people, whether of their own flesh and blood and honestly beloved, or strangers of each day.

I have always loved Ann Frank, always been deeply touched and saddened and inspired by her story. I suspect, however, that I would merely admire her, rather than love her, had she not twisted her heart inside out and upside down — not because of the dread of an unspeakably horrible kind of death — but simply because she knew how fine a person she could be, were there no other people in the world. I understand Ann very well, indeed, and very strongly suspect that almost everyone does who thinks about her. And I suppose I love her in part because she makes me feel like less of an ogre.

There Will Be a Candle

I was tucked away in an extraordinary seminary on the 9th and 10th of November in 1938. It was extraordinary in many ways, not least of which was that we were permitted no newspapers, no magazines, no radio (television was nonexistent). Had I known of *Kristallnacht*, I wonder if I could have stayed in the seminary over the next years, exempt from the draft which came later, particularly if I had seen the *New York Times* editorial of Nov. 11:

> In a day of terror (Nov. 9-10) surpassing anything even the Third Reich has seen, synagogues have been burned, shops sacked and looted, homes raided, a number of citizens beaten and thousands jailed. In Vienna a new wave of suicides swept over a people already broken and terrorized beyond endurance.

My friend Rabbi Haskel Lookstein describes *Kristallnacht* in *Were We Our Brothers' Keepers?* Elie Wiesel calls it a book "filled with painful accuracies." Rabbi Lookstein writes:

> One hundred and ninety-one synagogues were burned out. Over 7,000 Jewish businesses and shops were destroyed and looted. Nearly 100 Jews were killed, and thousands were subjected to wanton violence and sadistic torments. Many homes were devastated. Thirty thousand Jews were interned in Buchenwald, Dachau, and Sachsenhausen. The smashing of glass became the symbol of the destructive force of this pogrom and also gave it its name in history: *Kristallnacht*, the night of the broken glass. The amount of plate glass that was smashed that night equalled the entire annual production of the plate-glass industry of Belgium from which it had been imported.
> But more than Jewish store-front plate glass had

been destroyed. Jewish life in Germany was smashed
ruthlessly that night and in the month that followed . . .
This was all accomplished and reported widely in the
American and Jewish press by December 7, 1938.

I fear that I am not very patient with those who don't want
to remember. Now I'm going to say something shocking, that
many may protest. To say to Jews, "Forget the Holocaust," is to say
to Christians, "Forget the Crucifixion." There is a "sacramentality"
about the Holocaust for Jews all over the world. It constitutes a
mystery by definition beyond their understanding — or ours. It is
for many Jews the ultimate question about God in the 20th
century. Tread lightly, you who think you know, tread lightly and
be gentle in your thoughts. Speak of the Holocaust only if you
cannot speak of it without tears falling from your heart.

I am no more patient with Jews — less patient than with
Christians — who want the Holocaust forgotten. One Jewish
audience shocked me, traumatized me when I was new in town,
filled me with sadness when I had shared my own grief with them
over the Holocaust, and they made clear their utter lack of interest.
Perhaps some of them were among the Jews Rabbi Lookstein
describes as callous to events in Nazi Germany at the time of their
happening. Perhaps it is as painful for them to remember as it is
for the millions of Christians who ignored the slaughter.

A bitter line from Evelyn Waugh's *Put Out More Flags* comes
to mind. He was describing a fashionable dinner dance during the
war. "Fat wet bodies go glistening by." Why am I haunted by that
lonely line after 50 years? Wiesel puts it in his own way, in his
Foreword to the Lookstein book:

> The killers killed, the victims perished, and the world,
> though at war, did not intercede. Marriages and parties
> were held, daily prayers were recited, dinners and
> balls were organized: all this as though no flames were

consuming the heavens above a small Polish village
named Auschwitz.
Yet in America, they knew. Oh yes, they knew.

I write not to incriminate, but to plead. (Could anyone who
was protected as a seminarian not only from fighting in the war,
but even from reading about the war incriminate?) I plead and I
pray that *Kristallnacht* remembered 50 years later can help prevent
our forgetting what we knew as a people 50 years ago — or *that* we
knew.

There will be a candle in the window of 452 Madison Ave. on
the night of November 9th. I hope it will be one of millions burning
throughout our land — tributes to the human spirit the Nazis
could never extinguish.

"We Need a Revolution"

How can we have accepted it? How can we live with it as we
do? How can we shrug our shoulders, say no one has the answer
and there's nothing we can do about it?

Am I crazy that my bones ache with the agony of what drugs
are doing to us as a people? Am I out of my mind if I tell myself that
I must do something about it, even though it seems to be beyond
everyone's control? What should I do? Go parade up and down in
front of the house the *New York Post* wrote about, the "armed
fortress," with weapons too heavy for the police to dare entering?
Does it sound stupidly heroic to say I'd be perfectly willing to be
shot if it would end this monstrous ravaging of hearts and minds
and souls and bodies?

What do I answer when good, heartbroken people say their
kids, teenage and younger, are making hundreds of dollars a day
pushing drugs for the big bosses — money they never dreamed
existed?

Public officials tell me they can't interdict drugs, that there is no way of keeping them out of the country, the city, the little towns and villages, the bars, the classrooms. Police tell me that pushers are released as rapidly as they're arrested and simply laugh at the officer who arrests them. Judges tell me there's no way they can process the huge numbers arrested, no place to hold them, nothing to do but to turn them loose to ravage others.

Any single story smacking of scandal, or that is sexually salacious, stays on the front page of our newspapers and on our television screens for months and months on end. The daily destructiveness of drugs, the shattering of lives has become so commonplace that only an especially bizarre incident is given any media space. Some people have told me it's my responsibility to bring about a radical change in climate, a sense of outrage in all society. Simultaneously, I am told, it is my obligation to see that people are educated to what drugs do to them. It is assumed that constant, aggressive education is the primary response to the pushers, the thugs, the perverted criminals who rake in millions and millions of dollars by perverting others.

How does one do this in a society which has systematically purged itself of moral values? On what basis can a public school teacher tell students it is "wrong" to use drugs? Wrong is the opposite of right. It's a moral term. Teachers could get away with telling kids to use clean needles more easily than with telling them it is "wrong" to use drugs at all.

Why, indeed, is it wrong? One crucial reason is that every person is made in the Image of God. Play that on your secular piano! Why is it wrong to sell drugs to others who want to buy them? What responsibility do we have for others? Who said so? Teaching about the horrors of drugs necessitates teaching about the sacredness of human persons. Until we are prepared to accept that responsibility I believe the educational response will fall short.

Recently I read that some of the television networks have decided that "society's standards" have changed significantly so that they, the networks, can now plan to show more risque things, sexier things, more "adult" things. No sense of responsibility on the part of the networks, apparently, of what they have done precisely to change society's standards for the worse. No sense of willingness to say: "We have a responsibility to help preserve decent standards."

I am well aware that we can teach values and educate young people about drug abuse in our own Catholic schools and religious education programs. We do a good bit on drugs. We have an excellent program called ADAPP (Archdiocesan Drug Abuse Prevention Program) for our Catholic elementary and high schools. But how much time can one spend in formal educational programs, and how much of what we do is a finger in the dike against the flood of propaganda, pornography and general corruption? Our kids live in the real world, where peer pressure is tremendous, temptations are horrendous, and too many adults are far more self-indulgent than their children. What do we do about the actors and actresses whose public lives are essentially acts of contempt of every traditional value? What of those exorbitantly paid athletes whose drug use and childish behavior is excused on the basis of pressure?

An all-out onslaught against drugs is an absolute must in our society. When I served on the President's Commission on AIDS, I pleaded that we give maximum attention to drugs. The commission submitted a carefully designed 10-year program to the White House. When will it be seriously put to work?

If the New York police can't clean out the machine-gun-armed guerrillas in the crack houses — and I can certainly understand their problem — what of the National Guard? When will parents demand that school boards, legislatures, and courts authorize the teaching of moral values in our schools?

When will the Supreme Court recognize that the Constitution has been abused by the secularists who would rather see our kids' minds twisted and deformed through drugs than exposed to the traditional values that made our Constitution possible in the first place?

How much money are we putting into drug clinics, into drug abuse rehabilitation? In congressional testimony in the past, while urging a strong national defense, I have pleaded that the funding of at least some weapons systems be reduced in favor of housing. If we don't bring our drug problems under control, all the military force in the world won't assure our survival.

The situation is very, very bad. I can't hold my head up as Archbishop of New York unless I do everything I can about it. I don't know what that should be, but my bones tell me I have to work it through and pray it through fast.

Too many of God's precious people are being destroyed every day. We need a revolution in our society — a moral and spiritual revolution. I'm not talking about becoming a moral crusader, or trying to "Catholicize" New York. Indeed, I wish I could believe there were no "Catholic" drug pushers or users. But it's time to knock off business as usual. And it's time to stop looking the other way. That's how you get killed dead!

"What Are We Doing to the Young?"

I was hardly dressed for what was coming, in my miter, full vestments and holding my staff in hand, waiting outside Our Lady of Sorrows 125-year-old church to begin the anniversary Mass. Her look almost withered my miter. Her words withered my ears: "How many kids will die in these streets because you won't give out condoms in the schools?"

I could have shrugged it off as the no-win "When are you going to stop beating your wife?" question. I didn't. It disturbed me because she meant it and she was sincere. Nor is she alone in her thinking. Various school boards throughout the country are saying much the same, cheered on by editorials in some of the most important newspapers. I'm told a delegation of assembly-men from Albany want to come to see me to tell me that Catholic teaching on condoms is leading to genocide.

But now it would appear that the federal government itself wants to get behind condoms in a big way. I saw young kids on television enthusiastic over the idea; heard them say their parents should have nothing to say about it — "None of my parents' business."

Good God! What are we doing to the young? They are crying for bread, and we're giving them stones. Who is killing them, not only physically, but morally and spiritually?

I'm not going to argue that too many condoms are defective, or improperly used, or induce a sense of false security, so that kids end up with AIDS or a venereal disease or get pregnant. Those arguments are absolutely true, but there's a much more critical argument about pushing condoms on kids: It's wrong! It's corrupting thousands of kids. It's telling them they have no personal moral responsibility for their actions. It's telling them that the only real sinners are those who deny them condoms. It says: "It's not your fault if you get AIDS or give someone else AIDS. It's the fault of those who try to push moral values down your throats — those killers — those Catholic priests and bishops, those Protestants and Jews and Muslims who believe in Divine Law and personal responsibility."

William Murchison, syndicated columnist based at the *Dallas Morning News*, writes betimes for *The Human Life Review*. I quote from his article in the Summer 1993 issue, "The Straight '90's." Speaking of the striking down of a Louisiana sex-education curriculum by a state court, he writes:

> The curriculum recommends sexual abstinence as one means of preventing pregnancy and sexual disease. Ah, but the court reasons that the promotion of abstinence violates 'the taboo on interjecting religious beliefs and moral judgments into teaching.'
>
> Such a finding is as interesting as it is outrageous. What the court has done is concede to religion the high ground of common sense. In other words, it can't be

argued that abstinence doesn't work. Of course it works. Avoid sex, and you avoid the consequences of sex. But abstinence is also a moral proposition; in other words, morality equates with common sense. To do the right thing is to do the sensible thing, the thing that works. The court's problem is that moral connection. The Constitution (on the court's showing) rules out the interjection of moral and religious beliefs into public discourse.

This means, under the new order, we can't teach what works best. All we can teach is what works second and third best, such as condoms, which are notoriously ineffective in preventing pregnancy, much less AIDS . . .

. . . We rule out the best remedy as unconstitutional. We settle for runner-up remedies, not on account of their effectiveness but rather to facilitate the worship of ideological propriety.

I even hear otherwise intelligent people argue: "Well, kids are going to do what they're going to do, so at least we should give them *some* protection." And with that well-meaning "proverb" they buy into the "quick fix." Stop fighting the real problem. Give up on any hope of goodness and decency and common sense. Give up — let's face what we're really doing — give up on the antiquated notion that there's anything wrong with such normal good clean fun as sex outside of marriage, recreational sex, "inevitable" sex. "Everybody's doing it," so let's make it safe. It's *that* kind of "safety," not Catholic teaching on sex and marriage, on purity and virtue, on heaven and hell that kills. I have been scorned in some quarters before for saying it, but I'll say it again and again: "Bad morality is bad medicine." I have only heard that ridiculed, not disproved.

It's a sad, sad day when people really believe that the Church is engaged in genocide by teaching that condoms are a formula for disaster. It admittedly hurts to be called a killer, when you're all dressed up for Mass with a miter on. It hurts even more to know that others share that opinion. But it would hurt far worse if I believed it myself. Sorry, lady. I think you're dead wrong.

The Encyclical Is About Freedom

The funny thing is that when Sherlock Holmes told Dr. Watson that some marvelous hit of deduction he had used in his sleuthing was "elementary," it really was. Example from *The Sign of Four*: "When you have eliminated the impossible, whatever remains, however improbable, must be the truth." I recommend the process to those who want to read with an open mind the exquisitely beautiful encyclical of Pope John Paul II, "The Splendor of Truth." It's the process of a masterful theologian who is simultaneously a master of the spiritual life, and who has "eliminated the impossible" — the lies that have misled humanity into chaos — and offered us the freedom of truth that remains.

I would be amused, were I not saddened, by those who tell us that the pope just doesn't understand. He doesn't understand the subtleties of moral reasoning, they say, or the complexities of modern life, especially in the United States. Oh, but he does. Indeed, he does.

He not only understands — he *insists* on looking the realities of life smack in the face, dodging nothing. Not for him the evasion of a Pontius Pilate: "What is truth?" He knows that without truth there is only slavery. It is truth that makes us free, and truth alone.

What does Sherlock Holmes have to do with it? Take the "clean needle" issue raised by Earl Caldwell in the *Daily News* of Oct. 4, 1993. He quotes writer-researcher John Lauritsen who says, "It's all crazy," in regard to a proposal that the government distribute hundreds of millions of needles to drug addicts in an effort to prevent the spread of AIDS. Mr. Caldwell makes his own insightful comment:

There is a madness in all of this. The whole country is focusing on health reform. Yet the proposition now being put to the government (and to the taxpayers who will foot the bill) is that it is a good idea to flood the streets with clean needles as though that is any kind of answer.

Drugs tear the body apart. Clean needles or not, you end up with a person who is sick and broken and in need of care, and that means you have another burden in need of care. Health reform has to be made to mean something. Addicts have to be shown the damage drugs do to their bodies. And they have to know that the damage is coming, clean needle or not.

Clean needles are like condoms: a "quick fix" that makes matters a thousand times worse over the long run. With the widespread distribution of condoms has come the widespread promiscuity that has led to widespread teenage pregnancy that has led to millions of abortions. It's a vicious, vicious circle. And AIDS continues to spiral upwards.

Look at any issue of national or international concern, such as a national debt of unimaginable proportions, a public school system in unspeakable disorder, drugs completely beyond the control of government and police, gun battles and murders every day, meaningful health care beyond the reach of millions, poverty and squalor and political corruption that numb the mind. Look at a world torn by wars that never end, Bosnia being destroyed before the eyes of a helpless world, Somalia in terror, the Sudan seething, hundreds of millions starving across the face of the earth. This after the Holocaust, after genocide, after unutterable cruelties from which we seem to have learned so little. The way of falsehood and evil has not *worked*. It *cannot* work.

Isn't it time to eliminate the impossible? To turn resolutely from all that does not work? To turn, finally, to the truth?

Do we really believe the pope doesn't understand when he says so eloquently:

The splendor of truth shines forth in all the works of the Creator and, in a special way, in man, created in the image and likeness of God (cf. Gn 1:26). Truth enlightens man's intelligence and shapes his freedom, leading him to know and love the Lord. [n. 1]

And again:

. . . obedience [to the truth] is not always easy. As a result of that mysterious original sin, committed at the prompting of Satan, the one who is 'a liar and the father of lies' (Jn 8:44), man is constantly tempted to turn his gaze away from the living and true God in order to direct it towards idols (cf. 1 Th 1:9), exchanging 'the truth about God for a lie' (Rm 1:25). Man's capacity to know the truth is also darkened, and his will to submit to it is weakened. Thus, giving himself over to relativism and skepticism (cf. Jn 18:38), he goes off in search of an illusory freedom apart from truth itself. [n. 1]

No one can escape from the fundamental questions: *What must I do? How do I distinguish good from evil?* The answer is only possible thanks to the splendor of the truth which shines forth deep within the human spirit. . . [n. 2].

My copy of the encyclical, which is addressed to the bishops of the world for the guidance of their people, runs 179 pages, one more lyrical than another. As Peter Steinfels points out in the *New York Times* of Oct. 3, 1993, the text is far from being the fiery denunciation of "sex-related" conduct that reports had alleged in the previous few weeks. For example, the word "contraception" appears exactly once in this 40,000-word text. The attacks I had read before receiving the text itself made it out to be an entire encyclical on contraception. Indeed, I would call it an encyclical on freedom, on living as a truly free human person, basking in the light of the truth which makes us free. So, the pope says: "Only the act in conformity with the good can be a path that leads to life." [n. 72] Where does he get that? "If you wish to enter into life, keep the commandments." They're the words of Jesus found in Matthew (19:17).

What do those who would reject this encyclical have to offer in return? What political system or ideology has brought us freedom to be truly human, to be able to live in security, free from violence, free from fear, free from exploitation, from hunger and homelessness and war? As Thomas More asked, "And where has all good order gone among men if every disordered wretch can allege that his wicked deed is his destiny?" ["Law and Free Will"]

And yet, as with most documents from the pope that challenge us to turn from falsehood to truth in order to be truly human, much of this encyclical will be ridiculed, scorned, and rejected. Once again there will come an outcry to "shoot the messenger," not of bad news, but of good.

I suspect that Msgr. William B. Smith, professor of moral theology, is right on the mark (as he usually is) as quoted in the Steinfels report cited above: "[Our Holy Father] wrestles with every hot potato of the last 20 years in fundamental moral theology. For me it is a moral masterpiece. For others it may be a moral horror."

I'll go with the "moral masterpiece," this beautiful "Splendor of Truth."

"Why Don't They Ask Us?"

Ten faces look at me from a special Easter card. The front of the card reminds me that "He Is Risen!" Inside I am wished a Happy Easter and thanked for "Gift of Love," the residence on Washington Street run by Mother Teresa's Missionaries of Charity for victims of AIDS. Each photograph is signed.

I prop the card up on my desk where I can see it as I go

through stacks of technical reports on AIDS: programs, bro-
chures, proposals on treatment, research, prevention. I study the
statistics, the staggering costs of the massive educational programs proposed, the clinics, the condom distributions. I read the
publications of the blue ribbon committees, the learned advisory
panels, the conferences and conventions. I am told about single
partners, multiple partners, dirty needles, exchange of body flu-
ids, blood transfusions, intravenous drug use. I go from government proposals to medical proposals to educational proposals to
sociological proposals. Beneath all the terminology I sense des-
peration, moral bankruptcy and a frantic search for a "quick fix."

The 10 faces watch me. They seem to say: "Why don't the
researchers, the planners and programmers, the conferees and
educators and experts ask us? Why don't they ask what *we* really
believe, deep down, not merely about what we did, what contacts
we had, when we recognized symptoms? Why don't they ask us
if we think massive education about condoms or clean needles is
the answer? Why don't they ask us if exposing millions of youngsters to the sexual 'facts of life' from kindergarten through high
school is what preventing AIDS is all about?"

The 10 faces looking at me would want to know most
especially, I suspect: Who is talking about *love* in all these programs and proposals and multi-million dollar projects? Who is
talking about the kind of love many experience for the first time
when they go to "Gift of Love"? Who is showing in action the
gentleness, the understanding that they find in this simple little
house?

Or who, they would want to know, is offering a program that
allows for the power of *faith*, a faith that cannot be measured,
analyzed, or made a variable in an experimental design? The faith
they see in the little house on Washington Street?

What of *hope*, they would wonder. Where does it fit in the
array of condoms and clean needles?

Faith, hope, love: they're never mentioned in the mountains
of "scientific" literature on AIDS, and they are forbidden topics in
educational curricula on sex or on any other subject.

Many of our "Gift of Love" residents go to St. Vincent's Hospital before they die. There they find the same faith and hope and love. I visit them and am inspired. Many others go to St. Clare's, where we have the greatest number of beds devoted to AIDS patients, and where, once again, faith and hope and love are the most dynamic and visible elements of the treatment given. I'm sure the same is true in our other Catholic hospitals, all of which treat AIDS patients.

I don't know how many residents of "Gift of Love," if they had full physical life restored by way of miraculous medical treatment still unknown for AIDS, would engage in or return to activities that would lead to renewal of the disease. My suspicion is that the number would be very small indeed, not simply because they have experienced the suffering of AIDS, and certainly not because they have become experts in scientific knowledge or in the use of condoms, but because they have experienced the Gift of Love.

If faith and hope and love are good enough to help AIDS patients die in peace, might they not be good enough to help prevent people from getting AIDS in the first place? They cost a lot less than condoms.

"Talk to the Nurse About It . . ."

I felt foolishly guilty when told she had died while I was out of the country. There was no way possible for me to have been with her, and I knew that my "guilt" was sheer frustration.

I'll call her Therese, because at 23 she was in many ways a little child. That is, as I knew her. What kind of person she was before I first met her, when she was in a state of dementia, I don't know. Her memory was virtually gone, her ability to reason severely reduced. While much of the time she simply stared beyond space, she could be startled into acute anxiety. Yet I came to look forward to my visits to Therese, which were often late at night, when I could talk to her, whether or not she answered.

The fact was that for my first three visits in a row, she didn't answer at all, yet I believe deeply that she was hearing me. She had a small, pale, pretty face, with beautiful skin, always scrubbed gently but scrupulously clean by nurses or attendants. I would stroke her forehead and literally feel her anxiety lessen, even though she replied to none of my comments.

It was when I walked into her room during my third week of visits that she looked at me directly and said: "You're the cardinal." Were those words worth a million dollars to me? A billion? They were priceless, as was the very real, two-way conversation that followed.

"I want my hair washed," Therese told me. "It looks as clean as can be to me," I said. "No, it's not. They always promise to wash it and they never do." I felt her hair. "Why, it's still wet, as though it had just been washed," I said, "but, believe me, I'll talk to the nurse about it." "Promise?" "I promise."

I have seen the look on parents' faces, time after time, when they describe the first word out of their child's mouth. In my days of teaching retarded children, I have been as excited as their parents when a youngster would learn to tie a shoelace.

"You're the cardinal. I want my hair washed."

Therese was to recognize me on other occasions, not always, but gratifyingly often. It was undoubtedly the clerical collar that would remind her of pictures she had seen, and strike chords of memories from childhood. I didn't know until after many visits that she was Catholic. I never looked at a chart except to learn her name. She had AIDS, and that was all I needed to know. Others on the hospital staff, priest chaplains, sister pastoral ministers, were there to meet explicitly religious and sacramental needs. When patients with AIDS want to talk to me about their spiritual lives, I talk with them gladly. When they want me to pray with them, whatever their religious persuasion, I do so gratefully. Many do ask.

But much of the time Therese wanted to talk about the state

of her hair, and that, too, was fine with me. I had long since learned that her hair was, in fact, washed faithfully every day, and I had come to believe that this had simply become her way of starting a conversation with me, evoking my interest, testing my concern. She was obviously pleased when I would make a big fuss over her complaint, particularly when I would tell her that if somebody else didn't wash her hair soon, I would do it myself!

Then came the day that Therese wanted to tell me something of her life before AIDS; and I knew that she knew we had become friends.

I did have the privilege of being able to visit Therese very shortly before she died, to pray over and bless her, and to meet her own flesh and blood who clearly loved her. I knew she was dying, and I hated to leave. Her mother called while I was away and left word for me of her death. I was grateful for the thoughtfulness.

Therese never knew I had put her under the protection of St. Thérèse of the Child Jesus, the Little Flower, who died on a bed of excruciating pain. I knew it wouldn't matter to St. Thérèse how my friend had contracted AIDS. It would be enough that she suffered, and that in her suffering she became a little child.

I have offered the Sacrifice of the Mass for Therese, with great hope. A halo would surely convince her, once and for all, that her hair is forever as clean as a million stars in a snowfall.

In the AIDS Unit . . . Persons

I'd like to be able to sleep. A nurse once wrote an angry letter to a newspaper about me. I had just announced that I hoped to start visiting hospital patients with AIDS during the night, perhaps from midnight to three, because I'm a poor sleeper anyway. She wrote that if I were really interested in the patients, I'd go during the day, when help is needed. If I did a fraction of the work she does every day, she said, I wouldn't have any trouble sleeping.

She was right, of course, about the work. I'm sure she works

far harder than I do. Most people do. She was wrong about the
sleep. As a nurse she should know better. Insomnia has nothing to
do with work. It's a "disease." My mother was worse than I am.
She hardly ever slept, but she worked as hard as any nurse;
probably harder than a half dozen ditch diggers. In fact, she
worked a lot harder than my father, who was one of the world's
champion sleepers.

Actually I don't visit my patients in the middle of the night
because the hospital told me it wouldn't be practical. I try to go in
the evening; often I bump into family members that way. On the
evenings I visit patients, no matter how exhausted I am on arrival,
I come home wide awake. They are my worst non-sleeping nights.
I can't even read. I just worry and feel heartsick and try to pray.

The main thing I want to try to get across is that it's critical
that we recognize that persons with AIDS are *persons*, sacred
human persons, made in God's own Image. God loves them very
much. They may be in a state of dementia, staring into space,
bewildered. They may be disfigured with the lesions and tumors
and discolorations of Kaposi's sarcoma. They may be blind. Or
they may look and act like perfectly healthy people. Whatever . . .
they are *persons*, and those diagnosed with full-blown AIDS are
almost certainly going to die within months.

Some haven't had homes for years. Many who have acquired the disease through intravenous drug use have been living
in the streets, or on rooftops. They are virtually starved, terribly
feverish and, in many cases, desperately afraid. St. Clare's, St.
Vincent's, Cabrini and every other Catholic hospital in our system
welcomes them with open arms and open hearts, neither judging
nor condemning a single one. I myself have yet to ask one patient,
and I have visited and talked with well over a thousand, how he
or she contracted AIDS or what is his or her religion. It is enough
that each is a person.

I know there are many who cannot believe that the Church
can consider a given practice sinful, such as drug abuse or sexual
behavior outside marriage, or homosexuality, yet treat the "sin-

ner" as reverently as a saint. I read recently the minutes of a meeting of nuns in which, if the speaker was quoted accurately, the Church's teaching was grotesquely distorted.

For example, the speaker hopelessly confused the Church's teaching on homosexual "inclination" or "orientation," with the Church's teaching on homosexual actions. The former, of course, is no more sinful than any other inclination or temptation. The latter are sinful. The speaker as quoted implied that until a recent document issued by Cardinal Ratzinger, the Church rejected sin, but was compassionate to the sinner. The speaker suggested that Cardinal Ratzinger has turned that around and tells us to despise the sinner. What nonsense. Even the quickest reading of Cardinal Ratzinger's document makes crystal clear that this is precisely what the Church still teaches: love for the sinner, while rejecting the sin. Nothing has changed except in the mind of the speaker, who seemed intent on discrediting the Church and telling the women religious in the audience that it's time the Church learned something about compassion.

I wish the speaker would visit the archdiocese's "Gift of Love," run for us by Mother Teresa's sisters, or any of our hospitals, with nuns, lay doctors, nurses, ancillary staff people and volunteers working all sorts of hours, taking the pain of their AIDS patients home with them, weeping when they die — often dying, in part, with them.

The Archdiocese of New York is not yet doing enough, nor am I, personally. No one is. That's one of the things keeping me awake at night. It would keep me awake if I worked as hard as a nurse all day, or a ditch digger. And if that didn't keep me awake, the memory of the Christmas past that haunts me night after night, would keep me awake, just as it frequently wakens me and chills me and pains me, these months later. It's the memory of the 29-year-old man who died on Christmas day of AIDS acquired by IV drug use. His brother had died that same way a few months previously, his sister a few months prior to that. I cannot forget his mother that Christmas day, choking with grief at his bedside as he died.

That's the story I am telling our nuns and brothers and priests these days as I make my rounds of the workshops. I don't tell it to be dramatic. I tell it to remind them that AIDS is not simply acquired immune deficiency syndrome; AIDS is a sick person, a sick, sacred person.

Someone told me the other day that he has to "defend" me frequently from those who resent my teaching what I believe the Church teaches. His defense is that I am trying to help persons with AIDS to the best of my ability. The answer he purportedly receives is that I help them only because they are dying. The implication is, I was told, that I am happy because they die, while I go on hating those who live.

Would that keep you awake at night? Even if you're a nurse?

Gift of Love: You Have to Have AIDS

John Henry is not his name. He will die of AIDS but he will die happily in the Lord. He is one of those fortunate enough to live in "Gift of Love," the little house in Greenwich Village run by the Missionary Sisters of Charity. That means he is bathed in love.

I offered Mass for John on Monday of this week in St. Veronica's Church, to which the "Gift of Love" is directly attached. I confirmed him, too, and gave him his First Holy Communion. Maybe he has been happier in his life. I can't imagine when it could have been. On Monday his eyes were pools of joy. His shoulders were all bone when I put my arm over them. He is being consumed each day by the wasting disease.

But John's was no deathbed conversion. He is in full possession of his senses, knows precisely what he's about. He should have a number of months ahead, despite his wasting away physically, to continue his joyful growth in the faith he received not through fear, but through love.

A goodly number came to the Mass, local priests, Father Kevin O'Brien, episcopal vicar, Msgr. Joseph Snee, kind and generous pastor of St. Veronica's, seminarians, the residents of "Gift of Love," volunteers who assist the residents of "Gift of Love," laypersons like Mr. Richie Yezzo, administrator of St. Clare's, Missionary Sisters, including the entire community from the Bronx. Mother Teresa couldn't make it. That was all right. She's always present there, wherever she may happen to be physically.

I dropped in to see Ron. He was too weak to leave his bed for the Mass next door. I talked to him as I talk to all the helpless, reminding him that by uniting his helplessness with that of Christ on the Cross, he generates tremendous power for the world. It struck me that a few hours earlier I had said the same thing to a priest lying helpless on a hospital bed. We are all one in suffering. I had baptized Ron on Christmas Eve. He will spend this next Christmas in heaven.

Willie looked a little stronger than Ron, but he, also, was bedridden, too weak to come to the Mass.

He was in wonderful humor though. The room helped. Bright and shiny, clean as the sunbeams that poured through the sparkling windows. I can't get over how they can keep that old place looking so dazzling. As they mix love into everything else, they must mix it into their floor polish.

I keep coming back to that love because it's the wide-open secret of the place. There's only one absolutely essential entrance requirement to move into "Gift of Love"; you have to have AIDS. Being a Catholic won't get you in. You can be a Catholic, or a Muslim, or a Protestant, a Jew, a Buddhist, an atheist. What religion you are or how you got AIDS is irrelevant. The treatment is the same for everyone: a clean bed in a clean room, good food and a community of love.

Residents at "Gift of Love" want to bring things with them. So there are birds in cages and fish in a tank. There's no television because the Sisters want to create a community, where people talk with one another and listen and care — and don't simply turn on the television set to avoid learning how to really love other people.

When the confirmation and the First Communion had taken place and the Mass was ending, I told John Henry and everybody else what an honor it was for me to be part of it. That wasn't a cliche. For an hour and a half I had felt part of an ancient Christian community of spiritual brothers and sisters bonded by love of Christ, seeing Christ in one another, all awaiting the end of their pilgrimage, all anticipating being face-to-face with God.

Even as I was reminding John Henry that he was about to receive in Holy Communion the same Jesus Christ who had raised the dead to life, and was remarking that when He walked the earth, He could have cured AIDS by the touch of His hand, I knew that the gift John Henry had been given was infinitely greater than a cure of AIDS. The hand of Jesus had touched him with the gift of love — and of peace.

It's a remarkable little oasis, indescribably out of place in this violent world. It's there precisely because the world is so violent. It's there because, while the foxes have dens and the birds of the air have nests, the Son of Man in the man with AIDS so desperately needs a place on which to lay His head. He finds it there in that quiet, joyful little house. And men with AIDS find Him.

Priesthood and Religious Life

I Enjoy Being a Priest — And Why

I am so happy being a priest I can't imagine not being one. I love and admire many other people, and many times I envy them. Who wouldn't want to go home from work to a loving wife and children?

I envy doctors, and always wanted to be one — maybe a brain surgeon, or a psychiatrist, but probably a general practitioner. That's only the beginning of the list of would-like-to-be's. A lawyer? An archaeologist? How about a professional golfer? A university professor? A zoo keeper? A goldleafer like my father? A long-distance truck driver? An engineer on a train?

I'd like to be almost any of them, even simultaneously, and a lot of other things as well, like a chemist, or an astronomer, or a tugboat captain.

But trade being a priest? Not on your life.

One day when I visited residents in the new and beautiful St. Patrick's Nursing Home in the Bronx, I saw a lovely looking lady standing by her husband seated in a wheelchair. Every single day she goes to see him, without fail. My bones told me she needed a great big hug. She did. The tears flowed. "I needed that today," she said. "Thank you." How could I get to do that without being a priest? How could anything else make me so happy-sad?

Most every morning I have the 8 o'clock Mass in St. Patrick's Cathedral. I can't when I have a priest's funeral, or am off to Rome, or whatever. How I miss being there. Many of the same people come every day and newcomers, as well. They come from all over New York, because they work near the cathedral, they are tourists, vacationers, visitors for one reason or another. I get to know the regulars; to miss them, if they aren't there. I give them a three- or four-minute homily, or rather, I give *us* a three- or four-minute homily, because I need it more than they do. A few words of encouragement, of admiration.

How could I do without the Mass? It's my life. It's being a priest.

I don't get to hear the number of confessions I used to, but when I get a chance I jump at it. What a wonderful reminder of how good people really are. What a joy to be able to sit there and know how happy a penitent is going to be after confession, after you have talked with him or her, after you have given absolution. You know, because you know how happy you, yourself are after a good confession. I don't believe I have ever once given absolution to any one of the thousands of penitents whose confessions I've heard, regardless of what the person has done, that I haven't thought to myself what a wonderful gift this sacrament is — that a fellow as weak and human and sinful as I am can absolve somebody else's sins, and know that they are forgiven by God.

Being a priest can be confusing. Most priests are far too busy. They're pulled in a dozen directions at once. Somebody's dying in a hospital, there are prayers to be said at a wake, the school has to be visited, a couple wants to arrange a marriage, a mother wants you to go see her son in prison *now*, a shaken young woman insists she has to have an abortion, the parish council is meeting, two funeral Masses have to be offered, somebody at the door wants something to eat and a place to spend the night, it's time for baptisms — six babies. When are you supposed to say your prayers? When are you going to be able to close your bedroom door and get away from the phone, prepare a homily, go to bed before it's time to get up?

A priest can be lonelier than the howl of a coyote on a dark desert wind. It's an existential loneliness, the loneliness of Christ in Gethsemane, Christ on the Cross. It's a loneliness inseparable from the priesthood, a loneliness not even comforted by tears. A priest can also find himself bursting with joy over all the friends he has, the parishioners who love him, the students who think he's the greatest, the fraternity of priests — the strongest fraternity in the world.

I spend as much time as I can in preparing couples for marriage. Usually I keep them coming for about six months. I talk. I listen. I thrill over the fact that I have some 50 years of priestly experience to pass on to them, experience with couples entering marriage, experience with those already married — thousands of them. I cannot imagine talking to them so intimately about the spiritual, the emotional, and the sexual aspects of marriage, were I not a priest. They know I don't want to mislead them. They trust me because they know I love them. I'm their priest.

Then comes the wedding day, and I'm so much part of it I vibrate with their joy. And I pray for them, because I have seen thousands like them and many who haven't made it. Priests are for praying.

People can get terribly angry at a priest. He can't change a single one of the Ten Commandments to make life easier for them. He can't do a great deal about Church law to accommodate them. So they get angry at him — not really at him, but at the Church. He just happens to be the Church to them at that moment. It's part of being a priest. The disciple can't be greater than the Master.

I never bargained on being a bishop, and certainly not a cardinal. That's all right. I can still offer Mass every day, anoint the dying, bury the dead, visit the sick, house the homeless, feed the hungry, preach, baptize, hear confessions, witness marriages, pray — do everything I have been doing as a priest for so many years.

I love being a priest when I'm lonely and when I'm not, when I'm tempted and when I'm not, when I'm bone tired and when I'm not, when I wish I were a lot of other things and had a family of my own, when I think life will drag on forever and when I think I may die tomorrow.

I am awed in being a priest. I am awed in being a priest of the Archdiocese of New York. I would be awed in being a priest of a religious order, a missionary, a monk, a friar. For me, to be able to say over a piece of bread, "This is my Body," over a cup of wine, "This is my Blood" — that's the ultimate "power." It frightens me out of my wits, while it fills me with a wonder beyond anything else imaginable.

Pray for more priests and for the priests we have, and for

sisters and religious brothers and deacons who will serve faithfully. Pray for the lot of us on every day you get a chance. St. Matthew wrote well of what we're all about, and of what the critical needs are in the ninth chapter of his Gospel. It comes right before Jesus sends His apostles out on their first mission:

> Jesus went around visiting all the towns and villages. He taught in the synagogues, preached the Good News about the Kingdom, and healed people with every kind of disease and sickness. As He saw the crowds, His heart was filled with pity for them, because they were worried and helpless, like sheep without a shepherd. So He said to the disciples, 'The harvest is great, but there are few workers to gather it in. Pray to the owner of the harvest that he will send out workers to gather in his harvest.'

The Strength of the Priesthood Is His

There can be no doubt but that we priests leave a great deal to be desired. And we bishops. And we cardinals. You can never be quite sure what any of us are going to say or do. As I look back on my own years in the priesthood, I wonder how in the world God has tolerated me, or why He picked me in the first place.

Then I read again about Peter's denial that he had ever set eyes on Christ — while the cock crowed, "Peter, you're not only a liar, you're a traitor." I am reminded how James and John let their mother try to get Jesus to give them the top two spots in His Kingdom, and how it never dawned on Philip that Our Lord could feed a few thousand people without having to buy a shekel's worth of bread or fish. And poor Judas, Judas the thief, Judas the suicide.

Is it any wonder that Jesus lost His temper enough to call Peter, "Satan," and to tell him, "Get out of my sight"? Or that He had to shake His head with weary frustration and ask the very fellows He had personally selected, "How long have you been with Me, and you still don't know Me?"

That's all very encouraging to me. Oh, I'm sure it wouldn't be if they had all hanged themselves in despair, as Judas did. But they didn't. They didn't give up. Ten of the 11, after Judas had left, we are told, died as martyrs, Peter crucified, as was probably the case with his brother Andrew. Only John didn't die a violent death, but he did have to live out his days in exile on an island.

Even apart from their betraying Christ and running away from Him when their own lives were threatened, it seems to me that the Apostles were at least as unlikable as they were likable. I think of Peter arrogantly telling Jesus that He didn't know what He was talking about when He said He was going to be delivered over to His enemies. I think of how they fought among themselves over who would end up in first place. I think of the way they wanted Christ to obliterate a couple of towns — simply wipe them out with fire and brimstone from heaven. How did He put up with them? Were they the best He could come up with?

I have never known a priest, bishop or cardinal who would argue with a straight face that he was the best the good Lord could come up with. On the contrary, I suspect that most of us shake our heads in wonder that He called us, instead of countless millions who might well be better men than any of us even hope to be. What a mystery. What a profound mystery. What a *wonderful* mystery. That God chooses the weakest of the weak that the world may know that the strength of the priesthood is His strength, not ours. He gives us the awesome power to forgive the sins of others, so that the world may know that only by His crucifixion and death can *anyone's* sins be forgiven.

Who but a God with power beyond question would dare let men like us or *any* men demand that His power come into a piece of bread and turn it into the Body of His Son; into a cup of wine, and turn it into His Son's Blood?

Oh, how we tremble, we priests and bishops and cardinals,

not over what the press might say of us, or enemies might accuse us of, or friends might blame us for, but over our own awareness of our own weakness and unworthiness.

That's one reason why 700 of us gather in St. Patrick's Cathedral on Tuesday of Holy Week, at 5:30 in the afternoon, for the Chrism Mass, and reconsecrate ourselves to the Lord, rededicate ourselves to His people to the best of our all-too-limited ability.

The Chrism Mass is a wonderful time and place for such. With the consecration of the Holy Oils that every priest uses when he baptizes, the special oils the bishop uses when he confirms, or when he ordains priests, the oils we all use when we anoint the sick or the dying, we are reminded of the Sacramental life of the Church that we are so deeply privileged to serve.

I love the Chrism Mass. I love the priests who celebrate it with me, as I love the many others they represent who, for whatever reason, cannot join us in this very special Mass. I am grateful each year to be able to confess my own weaknesses publicly to my brother priests, and to ask once again for their understanding and forgiveness. I am grateful for that opportunity because I know they need and deserve a better bishop than I can ever be.

And they need and deserve all of you, God's good people. However they may have failed you or seemed to fail you, they love you. They want to serve you, and in overwhelming numbers they will be faithful to you until death, as the Apostles, all but one, became faithful to Christ unto death, even though they had failed Him so badly.

I cannot imagine a greater joy for the vast majority of our priests than to see you, God's people at the Chrism Mass. I even know a cardinal who would be euphoric to see you pack our beautiful cathedral that Tuesday — the second day after Palm Sunday, the fifth day before Easter. At 5:30 in the evening.

"If a Priest Could Cure Cancer . . ."

"I stole," I told the priest. I was 7. It was maybe my eighth confession. "What did you steal?" I fumbled for what might impress, or at least give my boast authenticity. "I stole a baseball bat and a box of candy." I hadn't prepared for a foxy reply: "Are you going to give them back?" The priest was an old-timer. He had heard kids' confessions before. He knew I couldn't give back what I hadn't stolen. That was better than 60 years ago, and I have never since fabricated a sin. The priest made his point. And then again, unfortunately, I haven't had to fabricate!

I'm not sure to this day why I made up such a story for the priest, but whatever the reason, it's obvious that although I probably *understood* what confession was all about, I didn't really appreciate it. That makes me one, I suspect, with a lot of people, not all kids.

I have asked the priests in New York to preach enthusiastically about the Sacrament of Penance or Reconciliation in Advent, to make penance services available where possible, and to do everything they can to promote a rediscovery of the beauty of this sacrament. And it is precisely its beauty that I'm not sure everyone appreciates.

Certainly one of the most beautiful scenes in the Gospel must be the description of Jesus' treatment of the woman caught in an act of adultery, dragged before Him, thrown at His feet. Only after He has shamed away her accusers because of their own sins, does He look at her. "Does no one condemn you? Neither do I. Go now, and sin no more" (Jn 8:3-11). In other words, you are completely free. You are truly liberated from your prison of sin. That's a truly beautiful thing.

What it seems to mean to the world when a people become free: a Berlin Wall is razed, an Iron Curtain is shattered, hostages are freed and returned to their loved ones. That's what the Sacrament of Penance or Reconciliation offers — that kind of lyrical freedom beyond anything the world has to offer.

When Dr. Viktor Frankl, a Jewish psychiatrist who later became a Catholic, was freed from a Nazi concentration camp, he wrote *Man's Search for Meaning*. In but a few sentences, he relives the first moments of freedom:

> One day, a few days after the liberation, I walked through the country past flowering meadows, for miles and miles, toward the market town near the camp. Larks rose to the sky and I could hear their joyous song. There was no one to be seen for miles around; there was nothing but the wide earth and sky and the larks' jubilation and the freedom of space. I stopped, looked around, and up to the sky — and then I went down on my knees. At that moment there was very little I knew of myself or of the world — I had but one sentence in mind — always the same: 'I called to the Lord from my narrow prison and He answered me in the freedom of space.'
>
> How long I knelt there and repeated this sentence memory can no longer recall. But I know that on that day, in that hour, my new life started. Step for step I progressed, until I again became a human being.

I am always taken by the story in St. Luke's Gospel about the paralyzed man carried to a house to see Jesus (Lk 5:17-26). The crowd around the house was so large they couldn't get in. So they climbed up to the roof, made an opening through the tiles, and lowered the paralytic on his pallet, right in front of Jesus. Seeing such faith, Jesus said to the paralytic: "Your sins are forgiven."

Immediately the unbelievers attacked: "Who is the man who speaks such blasphemy! God is the only one who can forgive sins." They were right — but they failed to recognize that Jesus had the power of God.

A lot of people fail to recognize that the priest has that very same power. The priest is unlikely to be able to do what followed in the scene from Luke. After Jesus had forgiven the paralytic's sins, He said: "Pick up your bed and walk." And the paralytic walked. But Jesus Himself made clear that forgiving the sins was infinitely greater than giving the power to walk.

That's part of what I mean about appreciating the Sacrament. I suspect that many of us would consider a priest a truly extraordinary fellow if he could miraculously cure cancer, give sight to the blind, hearing to the deaf, health to persons with AIDS. The poor fellow wouldn't have a minute's peace. People would come by the thousands and the hundreds of thousands day and night.

Strange that the same priest could sit in a confessional for hours or days and have only a handful of people come to be "cured" of their sins, restored from death to life.

Is it fear? Who should be afraid of mercy? Are we too busy? "What does it profit if one gains the whole world and loses one's soul?" Do we think confession is unnecessary? "Whose sins you shall forgive, they are forgiven," Christ said to His Apostles and the priests to follow them. Do we have the idea that receiving Holy Communion forgives our sins, regardless of what they be, and with no need for confession? Wherever we got that idea, it didn't come from the Church.

Surely it's not that we don't believe in sin? That really would worry me. I'd go back and read the first chapter of St. Paul's letter to the people of Rome. In effect, it says if we don't believe in sin, it's because we're wallowing in it — we've lost our senses of taste, sight, smell, hearing, and feeling. We no longer distinguish between good and evil.

The priest who asked me what I stole was a wise man. He knew I had stolen nothing, had not really examined my conscience, wasn't being honest. That may be one of the most common weaknesses of all. We may confess missing our morning prayers and say nothing about our heavy drinking. We may say we stole a newspaper, and not a word about maltreating employers or employees. We may confess impure thoughts and say nothing about hating blacks or Jews. Our understanding of justice may be that of a 7-year-old, though we are college graduates. Our Lord put it in the strongest words: "You hypocrites! ... you neglect to obey the really important teachings of the Law, such as justice and mercy and honesty ... You strain a fly out of your drink, but swallow a camel! ... You clean the outside of your cup and plate, while the inside is full of what you have gotten by violence and selfishness" (Mt 23:23ff).

Strong words from the Good Shepherd, but words that can change in the flash of an eye to, "This day you will be with Me in Paradise," the gentle response of the same Good Shepherd to the thief hanging at His side — the thief who had confessed his sins and asked for mercy.

"Shepherds After My Own Heart"

It is Tuesday, the 9th of March, 1993, and I am in Rome. I have just celebrated the Funeral Mass of a priest, Father Richard Mattie, in the chapel of the North American College. We served together as Navy chaplains. Last year he retired from the Navy after 20 years and had returned to his native diocese of Rochester, to serve in time as a parish priest. Prior to assuming such duties he had come to Rome for an extensive program of "updating" in theology and Sacred Scriptures.

Father Mattie was a gentle man, quiet, quintessentially good. As I sprinkled the water over this priest much younger than I, who I had assumed would bury me, I was reminded that this past Friday I had celebrated the Funeral Mass of Father John Fleming, in White Plains, the 200th priest of the Archdiocese of New York that I have buried in the past nine years.

I thought, too, that neither a Father Mattie nor a Father Fleming would ever have dreamed that in his lifetime he would see so much tragedy and scandal involving priests. The fact that the numbers have been fractional in comparison with the thousands upon thousands of priests in the United States does not lessen the scandal, nor does it alleviate for a fraction of a moment the pain of the victims of aberrations by priests, or the sufferings of families. The wounds remain open and raw for years, many scars never fully heal, many lives are permanently traumatized, many live henceforth in bitterness, some lose their faith. There can be, there should be, no denial of the damage done anyone: immediate victim, family, God's People, the Church, the priest himself.

And yet every year wonderful priests are ordained to serve God's People. The Fathers Mattie and Fleming are not singular, they are not exceptions. However many priests or even bishops may have become involved in or accused of grave or bizarre misbehavior, it is in no way a "cover-up" to reject the speculation that such is endemic in the priesthood. It is the sadness and the glory of the priesthood that every priest is human. It is sad, because, as a victim of Original Sin, he has inherited the same weaknesses, the same inclinations to evil that characterize every other human being in the world. Tempted in thousands of ways by the very nature of the occupational hazards of his daily life, a man, not an angel, he can slip and fall without warning, no matter how hard he has tried to be good, to be pure, to be holy.

The priest's humanity is likewise his glory, in that he understands temptation and even sin from personal experience. When I, myself, went to confession this past Saturday, the wise priest who listened to my sins gave me a beautiful penance: to meditate for 10 or 15 minutes on the 51st Psalm, the "Miserere." He understood my need because he is one with me as a priest. The 51st Psalm reads, in part:

> Have mercy on me, God, in your kindness.
> In your compassion, blot out my offense.
> O wash me more and more from my guilt
> And cleanse me from my sin.
>
> My offenses truly I know them;

my sin is always before me.
Against you, you alone, have I sinned;
What is evil in your sight I have done . . .

Make me hear rejoicing and gladness,
that the bones you have crushed may revive.
From my sins turn away your face
And blot out all my guilt.
A pure heart create for me, O God,
put a steadfast spirit within me.
Do not cast me away from your presence,
nor deprive me of your Holy Spirit.
Give me again the joy of your help;
with a spirit of fervor sustain me,
that I may teach transgressors your ways
and sinners may return to you.

Many have written beautifully of the "contrarieties" in the life of a priest; no one, perhaps, has written more insightfully than Emmanuel Cardinal Suhard, Archbishop of Paris some 50 years ago and founder of the Worker Priest movement in France:

As soon as the priest appears, passions crystallize, coalitions are formed. His presence suddenly releases pent-up feelings of aversion or of love. He is the touch-stone of consciences . . . This is the eternal paradox of the priest. He is a study in contraries. At the price of his own life he reconciles fidelity to God and fidelity to man . . . Until the end of time the priest will be the most beloved and the most hated of men, the most incarnate and the most transcendent; their dearest brother and their arch enemy! Until the end of time his mystery, which remains a holy enigma even to himself, will outlast world events and civilizations and be the great witness of the invisible kingdom . . .

Tomorrow evening I must give a lecture at the North American College on the latest message of our Holy Father on the priesthood. His message is called: "I Will Send You Shepherds." The title is taken from the book of the Prophet Jeremiah, of some 2,500 years ago. Jeremiah's world was in turmoil, filled with greed, corruption, injustice, and sexual licentiousness. God's answer was: "I will send you shepherds after my own heart, who will feed you with knowledge and understanding."

I will tell the listeners tomorrow night what I myself so deeply believe: that God will answer the needs of our day as He did those of the day of Jeremiah, and that I continue to believe profoundly in the shepherds He sends, who need our prayers so very much.

"We're Following the Leader"

It's a wonderful time to be a priest. Some people don't trust us. Some think we're in it for the money. Some think celibacy is a lost art. Some think we're a dying breed.

So there's no question about the challenge. And who wants to go through life without a challenge? There's no such thing as a free lunch. We have to prove our honesty, our integrity, our decency, our loyalty every step of the way, and every day all over again. One of us slips and falls and makes headlines, and we're all on trial. That may make life a bit tough, at times, but it's really high praise. It suggests that after nearly 2,000 years, people still expect us to be like Christ.

People have a good argument. Christ, Himself, was given to saying things to His Apostles like, "Be perfect, as your Father in heaven is perfect," and, "As the Father has sent Me, I also send you." That He held His Apostles to singular standards was made quite clear to anyone who wanted to join their company.

What Jesus knew very well, however, is that none of them would fully measure up; that they would all run away when it was time for Him to be crucified; and that the permanent failure rate for the first bunch He selected would be one out of 12. Poor Judas. He never really seemed to understand what Christ was all about. That's why he hanged himself. But in the meanwhile, 11 of the 12 came back, and when they did they came all the way: 10 to be executed for the faith, one to be exiled. Not bad on balance.

Another advantage to the challenge confronting us who are priests today is that we have to develop a lot of confidence in ourselves. Whatever other crises are plaguing the country today, there's no question about the crisis of confidence. A huge number of people not only have no confidence in others, they have none in themselves. We priests cannot afford the luxury of distrusting ourselves. We have to sail along serenely, however rough the waters or turbulent the winds. We have to believe we didn't call ourselves to the priesthood; we were called by Jesus, who knew what He was getting in us as He knew about the Apostles. "You have not chosen Me, but I have chosen you and appointed you to go and bear much fruit, the kind of fruit that endures." That's the same Jesus who reminded the Apostles when they thought their boat was sinking, "Why are you fearful? Do you still have no faith?" Then, we are told, "He got up and ordered the winds and the waves to stop, and there was a great calm."

Obviously, then, if we are to have confidence in ourselves, we have to have confidence in Jesus. And in His Church. For it *is* His Church. We didn't establish the Church any more than we called ourselves to be priests. The Church has taken a beating in every age, both from within and from without, as He guaranteed it would. And the Church is still very much here, as He also guaranteed would be the case. "And so I tell you, Peter, you are a rock, and on this rock foundation I will build My Church, and not even death will ever be able to overcome it." Which is a pretty good reason for us to feel confident.

Confidence is really a great gift. It helps us teach what should be taught, without equivocation, preach what should be preached, without ambiguity. It helps us comfort the sorrowing, feed the hungry, house the homeless, forgive the sinner, for we know that it's really the Lord doing what He wants done through us. We can slip and fall and pick ourselves up and start all over again. We know where we are going, because we're following the Leader, who was very explicit in telling us, "Come, follow Me."

The United States Marine Corps recruiters used to have a great slogan, and perhaps still do: "We don't promise you a rose garden." I don't want to be irreverent, but Jesus never promised any garden but the garden of Gethsemane, where He sweat blood knowing He was about to be crucified.

Isn't it marvelous that He makes the same offer today, and that men of our day still take Him up on it? That takes a lot of confidence today, and a lot of faith. Nobody with any sense scrimps and saves and works and studies and sacrifices for years to join the crew of what he sees to be a sinking ship. Nobody in his right mind puts out to sea with a bunch of thugs and cut throats. It seems to me that the men who will become priests these days have a more than adequate understanding of what they are about and why — and whom they're signing on with, and in what kind of a ship.

In one of her pungent letters to "A.," Flannery O'Connor talks a bit about the short story that escalated her into literary fame, *A Good Man Is Hard to Find*, and asserts: "My audience are the people who think God is dead . . . As for Jesus' being a realist: If He was not God, He was no realist, only a liar, and the crucifixion an act of justice."

No doubt about it, a good man is hard to find, but the good men who are called to the priesthood are realists who believe that Jesus was no liar.

Passionately convinced that He is the Son of God and that He has called them, they are totally committed to follow. If any of them — of us — get a little bit lost at times, or follow a more crooked path than He walks, most keep slogging ahead on the straight and narrow, and even many who have strayed one day find the way back, and even many of the folks they may have hurt or misled forgive them and are glad to see them back where they belong. People are truly extraordinary, and you can never underestimate their goodness.

"The Heart Has Its Reasons . . ."

Why in the world would anyone want to become a priest today? Talk about passage on the Titanic. . . !

Try two young medical doctors, two law students, one MBA, one graduate student getting an MBA, one school teacher. I recently had dinner with all of them. They wanted to talk about how to become priests. They had some questions about tailoring programs of spiritual formation and studies in theology to try to meet their current circumstances. They had further questions about the use that might be made of their professional skills after ordination to the priesthood. They had no questions about the priesthood itself, nor about their own desire to become priests. It was my second meeting with them. It was not a flash in the pan.

They are very alert young men, chiefly in their late 20's. They know the stories of the latest scandals in the Church as I do. They have read the headlines, seen the pictures, studied the accounts. They still want to be priests, highly educated priests, holy priests. We talked about that. They don't want shortcuts. They're not looking for an easy road to ordination. They reject any watering down that would make them second-class theologians. They listen carefully when I tell them that as much as we want well-educated priests, we want holy priests even more. They understand.

So what's wrong with them to want to identify themselves with a breed that speculators expect to be extinct by the end of the century, with others suggesting that's not nearly soon enough? The answer's easy if you believe in mystery. That's what a vocation is: a mystery. It defies all human reasoning, or, as Pascal put it: "The heart has its reasons that reason never knows."

Why did I become a priest nearly 50 years ago? Because it was a popular thing to be? It was, in some circles, but that's the last thing my classmates or I thought of. I suppose we all felt pretty much the same way, however we might have tried to articulate it: we wanted to help people get to heaven and do whatever good they were able to do along the way. We wanted to tell people about God, to preach them the good news called the Gospel, to forgive their sins, witness their marriages, baptize their babies, comfort them in dying. We wanted to do the holiest thing we could possibly do — celebrate Mass and give people the Body and Blood of Christ. We wanted to teach, to work in parishes, to take charge of altar boys and the Sodality and the Holy Name Society. We wanted to feed the hungry, temporally and spiritually.

Where did we get all that? From our families? From books, teachers, priests? Certainly some of these may have been circum-stantial, but not one, not all, could have brought us to the day of ordination. Our Lord was exceedingly clear about that: "You have not chosen Me, but I have chosen you, and have appointed you that you should go and bear fruit, and that your fruit should remain . . ." (Jn 15:16).

Without a shred of false humility, I can say categorically that had I been the Archbishop of Philadelphia, who ordained me to the priesthood, I am the last man in the world I would have ordained, the least likely, in a thousand ways! Nor can I pretend to pinpoint with any accuracy what really motivated me to apply for the seminary, or why seminary authorities accepted me and passed me on, year after year, until the big moment came. None of which is to speak any more disparagingly about myself than what I could say about the Twelve Apostles Christ chose origi-nally. Peter was a bumbler and a coward, James and John had terrible tempers, Philip was naive, Thomas a skeptic, and so on, with Judas Iscariot, the ultimate deceiver, home of the father of lies.

What a profound mystery, Christ's calling the Apostles. It's the mystery of the call of every priest ever since and of every priest to come until the end of time. It's the mystery of two medical doctors, two students of law, one master of business administration, one graduate student thereof, one school teacher. If they become priests, it will be because He has chosen them, not because they have chosen Him.

I told them I would write this, because they believe there are many more like them "out there." I happen to share that belief and am prepared to stake a meal on it, in which at least seven young gentlemen are prepared to share. Soon or late we'll come up with a formula to put the priesthood within their grasp, if God wants it that way.

Thinking of the priesthood and hungry? Write me a letter (1011 First Avenue, New York, N.Y. 10022) or give me a call (212-371-1000). I'm around.

New Signs Of Hope

After the 10 o'clock Mass in St. Patrick's on Sunday, December 2, 1984, I had a cup of coffee with Sister Melinda Roper, just finishing up as president of the Maryknoll Sisters. A number of other sisters joined us, as did Bill Ford and his family, and some other laypersons.

They had all come to the Mass in honor and memory of the four American missionary women killed on the same date four years earlier in El Salvador. Bill's sister was one of them, Sister Ita Ford. Sister Maura Clarke was another. They were both Maryknollers. Sister Dorothy Kazel, an Ursuline, and Miss Jean Donovan, a laywoman, were the other two. I preached about them on Sunday, about them and the countless numbers of heroic people like them. The lives and deaths of these four beautiful women are a precious example to me. But here I want to talk about the hundreds of thousands of women they represent, and especially the women religious of the Archdiocese of New York.

I have seen a good bit of those women since I have been here.

In a first go-around I had Mass and a talk for each of the five different groupings of them — probably a total of 2,000. Then I held a series of "listening sessions," again in five different groupings. This time the sisters did the talking.

But quite apart from such formal get-togethers, I have seen them at work all over the archdiocese — in soup kitchens on the Lower East Side, in the South Bronx and in the counties of the north, in hospitals and classrooms, nursing homes and schools for the handicapped, in shelters for the homeless, employment projects for the jobless. I have seen them opening their hearts to pregnant, unmarried teenagers, their arms to new babies, in every imaginable kind of advocacy program for the poor, in spiritual institutes for minorities, counseling for the "advantaged" and the "disadvantaged," in prayer groups and study groups, in prisons. I have seen them reaching out to addicts, drunks, alcoholics, to the confused, the disoriented, the psychotic. Remarkable. Remarkable sisters.

They are different, some of them, from the sisters who taught me as a youngster, and some of them are exactly the same. Many have advanced academic degrees in an extraordinary variety of disciplines and experiences broader than some of their counterparts 50 years ago might have thought possible. Some dress "traditionally," some in more contemporary garb. Many live in convents and monasteries and big communities, some — not a great number — in apartments on their own. But I find myself absolutely awed by what these women do and by what these women are. Perhaps the highest praise I can pay them is to say, with considerable sadness, that there aren't enough of them — not nearly enough.

I believe, however, that one of these days, and sooner than a lot of us may believe, we're going to experience a new springtime in vocations among our women religious. It has to be. There are far too many fine young women growing up these days with glowing ideals and a deep hunger to serve others to be pessimistic about what they will do with their lives. And the more they learn about the thousands of sisters pursuing those ideals in the Archdiocese of New York, and pouring out their lives day after day, the more the likelihood, in my judgment, that a lot of young women will want to follow in their footsteps, in the archdiocese, in Africa, in Asia, in Latin America, or wherever God calls them.

This is the kind of optimism inspired by a Sister Ita and a Sister Maura, a Sister Dorothy and a Jean Donovan and by the thousands right here at home who make me proud and humble to be the Archbishop of New York, and bursting at the seams with hope for the future.

They "Help God to Create Others"

Can I really get away with saying I almost became a Trappist monk, without everybody who knows me getting hysterical? In my almost-became-one day Trappists never talked! They took a vow of silence. Will anybody who knows me today believe that that's precisely why I almost signed up?

The first temptation to become a Trappist came so long ago that a round-trip bus ticket between Philadelphia, Pennsylvania and Providence, Rhode Island, cost $8. I must have been all of 18 years old and had been reading the melodramatic but exceedingly impactful books of Father M. Raymond, Trappist monk. One was *The Man Who Got Even With God*. Another, as I recall, was *Burnt Out Incense*.

Our Lady of the Valley Trappist monastery was in Valley Falls, Rhode Island, a few miles outside Providence. I was determined to visit. I made $5 of the $8 by selling an undistinguished poem to *Columbia* magazine. Some odd job must have earned me the other $3.

Our Lady of the Valley was not nearly so romantic as Father Raymond's books. The guest house was authentic American primitive. I was given a bunk in a room with five men. When the monastery bells bonged at 2 a.m., I hadn't yet closed my eyes, but followed the men to the monastery church, where the monks chanted Matins, or morning prayers, in almost total darkness. It had to be at least 4 a.m. when we got back to our room, and the big bells bonged again at 5 a.m. to call us back to the church.

Father Michael, the guest-master, had been a Royal Canadian Mountie who looked nothing whatsoever like Nelson Eddy. As guest-master, he was allowed to talk, but he clearly didn't find me interesting enough to talk to. He put me in the kitchen, peeling potatoes. After three days I was an unmitigated zombie and couldn't wait to leave. I hated it. A few years later the monastery burned down with no help from me, and the Trappists moved to a magnificent 2,200 acre property in Spencer, Massachusetts, where they still hold forth.

Yet Our Lady of the Valley had tricked me. I left there convinced I never wanted to see it again. A couple of years later I was writing to the prior to tell him I wanted to sign up. He wrote a gracious letter telling me to come ahead. Why I didn't go is too personal a story to be of any interest to anyone but myself.

Then why do I bring it up after some 50 years? Because four contemplative sisters came in to see me the other day. The years flew away, and I knew that I have never lost my belief in the enormous power of the contemplative life. They were from four different congregations, all with houses here in the archdiocese. Their primary business is to pray.

Years ago, as confessor to a beautiful young woman whose talents were already winning her a series of smashing successes, I agreed with her decision to enter a contemplative congregation. Practically everyone we both knew thought she was crazy, and that I was even crazier for encouraging her. "What a waste," was the cry, "what a waste."

They were right, of course, if spending a large part of your time talking to God and listening to God is a waste. They would probably be right, too, if they called it "un-American." I sat once on a Saturday afternoon in a forest in Vermont, where Father Boylan, a Carthusian from Ireland, was trying to turn some

Americans into Carthusians. The rain was beating on the tin roof of his hut and the whole world of the forest seemed to me dismal when he told me: "Most Irish and Americans are not temperamentally attuned to the contemplative life."

Maybe "most" aren't, but more are than one might guess, such as my lovely, talented young friend, who has been a contemplative for over 40 years now, and I can't count the scrapes her prayers have pulled me through. She has never believed she has "wasted" her talents.

We have a variety of contemplative sisters in the archdiocese: Discalced Carmelites, Poor Clares, Redemptoristines, Monastic Sisters of Bethlehem, Sacramentine Nuns, Dominican Nuns of Perpetual Adoration, the Missionaries of Charity, the Maryknoll Cloister and the Contemplative Sisters of the Good Shepherd. They keep me going. Without them, I'm convinced, every problem in the archdiocese would be a thousand times worse — drugs, AIDS, homelessness, hunger, violence, racism, name it. They work miracles of grace, seven days a week.

There is room in each contemplative congregation here in New York for those called to the apostolate of contemplation. And an apostolate it is, not an escape. One doesn't become a contemplative to escape the world, but to help save it.

In his *Seeds of Contemplation*, the famous Trappist Thomas Merton observes: "We become contemplatives when God discovers Himself in us." And in the same work he tells us: "The poet enters into himself in order to create. The contemplative enters into God in order to be created." Father Merton would probably not mind my adding to "in order to be created," the words, "so that he/she can help God to create others."

"Answer to the Siren of Death"

Seventeen they were, in all, each offering, as Mother Teresa of Calcutta would put it, "something beautiful for God." Schoolteachers were among them, and a legal secretary and a librarian; a number of nurses were there and a freelance editor and two medical doctors, a lawyer and a senior in college. All were making the four-day, four-night discernment retreat I conducted in early November, 1991. All were deeply interested in our Sisters of Life. God alone knew at that time how many would apply for the new "class" to begin in February, but that they would come from all over the land to make such a retreat was itself a great gift.

It was hard to tell on Sunday during the retreat who impressed whom more: the 17 retreatants or the eight Sisters of Life postulants who came to visit them. I take that back. *All* of them impressed me profoundly. The eight who had been five months, day and night, in spiritual formation, prayer, study and the plain hard work of trying to form a community out of one-time complete strangers had made amazing progress. Their joy was catching.

I watched and I marveled at the interchange and at what the Holy Spirit seemed to be doing. The 17 retreatants from the deep South and the Southwest, from Canada and New York, from California and Washington, had come to the retreat with only their faith and their commitment to the cause of human life in common. Then they began to pray together, to receive the Eucharist together, to listen and talk and laugh and think and worship together. In a handful of hours they had begun to congeal, but ever so tentatively, still asking themselves almost furtively if they could ever truly live together and work together and love God and His most vulnerable ones together for the rest of their lives. The advent of the eight postulants gave them amazing hope.

The eight Sisters of Life postulants, too, had come from an extraordinary diversity of backgrounds, and from all over the land. They had come, in some cases, against the reluctance of their families, the jibes of their associates, the head-shaking of their friends. They, too, had come primarily because of their deep concern over the widening and intensifying threats to human life in our land. About such threats they were thoroughly knowledgeable. It was the "how to respond" that perplexed them. So for the past five months they responded primarily with prayer.

This was what became almost startlingly clear to the 17 retreatants as I watched and listened. They recognized that they were actually hearing eight real-life, emotionally balanced, well-educated, healthy, vigorous women talking about how they take the cruelest problems of the world to Jesus in the Blessed Sacrament, and find themselves at peace in the doing. It was obvious to the retreatants that each of the postulants had been an activist in the world, each with her own ideas about how best to protect and enhance human life, each engaged in the struggle. These now are the women who have come to believe passionately that whatever activity is to prosper, it must be rooted in prayer.

The eight postulants, in turn, saw themselves in the 17 retreatants. They knew the struggle and the perplexity of being confronted with an invitation to "Go, sell what you have and give to the poor, and come follow Me." Now living the way of poverty, chastity and obedience themselves, they knew well what it is to invite others to follow. So they were respectful of women opening themselves to the Holy Spirit, asking God to tell them what He wants of them, then give them the grace they need to respond.

Our retreat was still under way when word came of the poor man who purportedly killed himself by asphyxiation in his own car. We were saddened and we prayed. We prayed even more fervently when we heard that Derek Humphry's book *Final Exit* was in the suicide car, spelling out precisely the procedure that leads to death. We prayed so very fervently because we believe prayer to be the only answer to the utterly irrational, the only response to the siren of death that is bewitching our land — prayer and penance and the giving of one's life that others will live and let live.

All This in Silence . . .

The Winter's Tale should be better known than it is, so filled is it with modern hatreds and lusts, suspicions and senseless violence that can be redeemed only in silence. I know by heart but a single line of this early 17th century work of Shakespeare, but for me it's the heart of the play:

> The silence often of pure innocence
> Persuades when speaking fails.

They would have been embarrassed had I said so, but it was the silence of pure innocence that I was listening to as each of nine contemplative nuns "reported" to me the nature of their lives. Each of a different contemplative community in the Church of New York, they had come with their sisters to spend those hours with one another and with me that I have come each year to cherish. "How could you think you see in us pure innocence?" they would have asked. "We are women, flesh and blood, not alabaster statues."

And I would have affirmed this freely, for these are, indeed, women of intense passion. They love deeply, with a love fully expressible only in silence, and their silence is made "pure innocence" by the One they love.

In his lilting, book-length poem, *A Woman Wrapped in Silence*, John W. Lynch describes the visit of the shepherds to Bethlehem, to "find the infant wrapped in swaddling clothes, and laid in a manger." They went at the bidding of angels to see:

> And still was here a woman
> Wrapped in silence, and the words were closed
> Within her spacious heart for pondering.

The nuns telling me of their lives in this ultra-modern era were light years removed from the stereotypes of "Come to the

Stable," lovely as was Loretta Young those days in her Hollywood sisterliness. Nor were they the helpless flutterers desperately in need of rescue by Whoopi Goldberg in her "Sister Act." They might have been my blood sisters, who have reared many children and still miss their deceased husbands. They might have been lawyers in the famous corporate firms of Manhattan, doctors in sprawling city hospitals, social workers or secretaries or department heads in Catholic Charities or the Chancery. They were, they are, very normal women.

But they are different. They are wrapped in silence. Their "pure innocence" is not that of Mary, conceived in innocence, but a derived innocence, the innocence of intimacy with the One conceived in the silence of a womb filled by the Holy Spirit and born in the silence of a cave. No matter that they are women tempted as all of us, women who may sin at any moment as all of us. They are women who have made their choice to love recklessly, with total abandon, in order to redeem the world in silence.

For the world is a noisy place and full of the sounds of sin. People kill one another and violate one another and hate and lust after and exploit one another. "With desolation is the world made desolate," mourns Jeremiah, "because no one *considers* in his heart." But these women *do* consider in their hearts. They pray for the world in their silence and by their silence.

Yet their laughter is fresh, these women of contemplation who bear their own sorrows. They are not solemn; they are simply holy, with a holiness that is totally realistic in the tradition of the little Thérèse of Lisieux and the great Teresa of Avila and Francis and Clare of Assisi and of so many others who have known that they could only save the world by giving it up. St. Thérèse said it for all of them, or at least for extended periods in the lives of many — the price they pay for souls:

> God allowed my own soul to be plunged in thickest gloom, and the thought of Heaven, so sweet from my earliest years, to become for me a subject of torture. Nor

did the trial last merely for days or weeks; months have passed in this agony and I still await relief. I wish I could explain what I feel but it is beyond my power. One must have passed through the tunnel to understand how black is the darkness.

. . . But dear Jesus, Thy child believes firmly that Thou art the Light Divine; she asks pardon for her unbelieving brethren and is willing to eat the bread of sorrow as long as Thou will it so. For love of Thee she will sit at the table of bitterness where these poor sinners take their food and will not rise from it till Thou givest the sign. But may she not say in her own name and in the name of her guilty brethren: 'O God, be merciful to us sinners.' Send us away justified. May all those on whom faith does not shine at last see the light! My God, if that table which they profane must be purified by one who loves Thee, I am willing to remain there alone to eat the bread of tears until the day when it shall please Thee to bring me to Thy kingdom of light. I ask no other favor beyond that of never offending Thee.

All this in silence, all in contemplation.

The Year — Religious and Secular

Advent:
It Was the Color Purple

Advent was more of a feeling in our house than a liturgical season. Neither my mother nor my father could have talked comfortably about "liturgy." You went to Mass, not to a "liturgical celebration," as meaningful as the latter term is to those who understand it.

You did some penance in Advent, but not big-league stuff, as in Lent. Advent penance was like what St. John the Baptist called for in the desert — penance all mixed up with joy: "Repent, for the Kingdom of God is at hand." In other words, get ready, clean things up, the Messiah is here.

With complete respect, "Messiah" was another term my folks wouldn't have been big on, especially my father. With him it was "Christ," never even "Jesus," alone, which he would have considered presumptuously familiar.

We were all big, though, on the "waiting" part of Advent. This was years ago, before the Christmas season started on the day after Thanksgiving. Christmas was Christmas. Thanksgiving was Thanksgiving, marked by the big Thanksgiving Day "Gimbel's Parade." That's when I first got blood poisoning through my heel.

I was only a little kid marching with the St. Clement's parish band, alternately playing a fife, a bugle, and a drum. I was a menace on all three, which is undoubtedly why they kept switching me from one to another. The old-fashioned stiff canvas leggings were at least six sizes too big for me, and hit and scraped between the top of my shoe and my heel, all the way up Philadelphia's Broad Street.

One night floating in a mud hole in the side of a hill in Vietnam, I began to feel sorry for myself, telling myself I had never been so miserable in my life. Then I remembered Broad Street on the coldest Thanksgiving Day in history with the bottom edge of that diabolical canvas cutting into my heel. I fell asleep happily wallowing in the soft wet mud.

But Christmas was a long way off: weeks of waiting. The first Sunday of Advent, with its purple vestments, was the first sign to be taken seriously. There was something about that purple. It made a little boy feel sad and solemn and glad all at the same time. Perhaps I was old enough to relate it to the purple of Lent and the purple robe they put over the shoulders of Christ, when they mocked Him by calling Him a king after beating Him to a pulp. It wasn't to be for many years that I would learn that in his Gospel St. Luke used the same Greek word for the wood of the Cross on Calvary that he had used for the wood of the manger in Bethlehem. So my relating Advent to Lent was hardly an intellectual achievement; it was the color purple, I think, and maybe that I felt something of the same kind of joy over the coming of Christmas as the coming of Easter. After all, it was the same One coming on each occasion.

But there was definitely a difference between Advent and Lent in our house. My mother, who was a world class faster from sweets during Lent, felt nothing of a similar obligation during Advent. I suspect her penance may have been in worrying what she was getting us for Christmas. Her problem wasn't that we were the kids who had everything. We had little, and she had even less, including money. And it wasn't something she could discuss very fruitfully with my father. He would suddenly become intensely interested in the sports pages, and utter reminders she didn't need about how lucky we kids were in comparison with the starving babies in India. It wasn't at all that he was a skinflint. He would literally give us the shirt off his back. It was that he saw this as my mother's job, and he could be very big on job classifications!

Fasting or not, however, they both *felt* Advent. My father would be very faithful, for example, to that beautiful little Advent prayer: "Hail and blessed be the hour and the moment at which the Son of God was born of the most pure Virgin Mary, at midnight, in Bethlehem, in the piercing cold. In that hour, vouchsafe, O Lord, to hear our prayers and grant our petitions, through Christ Our Lord." Simple. Adventish.

So we waited, and when we were *very* little, the hoped-for advent of Santa Claus was very much part of it all. But even at our tiniest we were made to feel very comfortable that if Santa didn't bring a great deal with him, or didn't even come, the Christ Child would be there, and that He was Christmas. I'm not fancying that merely in retrospect, after years and years have long faded into the faintest of recollections. The Christ Child *was* Christmas in our house. That is as fresh today for me as at the age of 3 or 4. And when First Holy Communion time came, it was Christmas all over again, without the tinsel, and in the shadow of a tree called the Cross.

The same One was being born in our souls who had first been born in Bethlehem.

I don't know how they were able to teach us such things in those days — things never forgotten. My father and mother weren't theologians, nor were the sisters who taught us our catechism. But both my parents and the sisters succeeded in teaching without even trying. Almost certainly because they believed and felt what they taught.

Christmas:
Ringing the Bells for Santa

Every 4-year-old should have a 9-year-old sister with a vivid imagination who can tell outlandish stories with outrageous believability. Only thus could it happen that while you're lying awake in your trundle bed on Christmas Eve, being stiller than a dormouse while straining to hear the beat of the reindeer, such a sister could come into your room and tell you Santa Claus is downstairs in the kitchen with his white whiskers caught in the gas range! That's the kind of sister I had at 4. I have never since been able to envision a Santa Claus without a tangled beard.

There's significantly more to that absolutely true story than that I wasn't a very bright 4-year-old. What's remarkable about it to me is that it didn't shake my belief in Santa Claus and hasn't done so to this day. Nor did I ever doubt that Santa Claus came from the North Pole. Where else *should* he have come from, looking as he did?

Of course, apart from Christmas Eve, the real Santa Claus could be found only at Gimbel's, in Philadelphia, on the Saturday after Thanksgiving. Then he went back to the North Pole to get ready for Christmas. We were never exactly told that the real Santa Claus was not in Macy's, in New York. We were simply not told that there was a Macy's. Or a New York. So I can remember sitting on Philadelphia Gimbel's real Santa Claus's lap quite as vividly as I can remember processing down the long center aisle of St. Patrick's Cathedral to be installed as the Archbishop of New York well over a half century later.

I'm not quite sure, but I suspect my ease with the notion of Santa Claus has to do with the way my mother and father taught us the meaning of Christmas — never superstitiously, but always imaginatively. The infant Jesus, of course, was at the heart of it all, with Mary and Joseph absolutely indispensable (only with Joseph a little less absolutely indispensable than Mary, for reasons they taught us when we were ready to learn them). Then came the shepherds and the angels —very real angels with a very real story to tell. There were always sheep and cattle, even if they reposed on green crepe paper, sprinkled with sparkling "snow," inevitably a sheep dog, and three Wise Men, one black. Two stood respectfully off to the side; one knelt.

It never seemed the slightest bit incongruous to us that this full display of heavenly and earthly creatures was positioned in and around a stable placed immediately next to, if not even within, a little circle of train tracks that ran around the Christmas tree, featuring little paper box houses and a church with a steeple (with an electric tree bulb inside). We knew the secret. The Christ Child was not simply born on a Christmas Day some 19 centuries ago; He was a member of the family in our tiny little row house in Philadelphia. He was quite as real to us as He could ever have been to the shepherds. We hadn't even heard the *word* in those days, but there was never a question of "irrelevancy." He could lie quite as peacefully in a miniature manger in our living room right next door to the railroad track and the Currier and Ives paper box cutouts, as He did in a stable in Bethlehem, for that's the way He is, we were taught.

After all, my now long-departed and faithful mother and father gave me to believe, He was not only a little baby like every baby — He was God's baby. Indeed, He was God Himself, even though He was only a little baby. A story so wondrous just had to be true. We never had a problem with it. We have never had one since. Their teaching was marvelous, undoubtedly because they believed so very thoroughly and beautifully everything they taught us.

And somehow there was room in it all for Santa Claus. After all, why *wouldn't* God send somebody around to celebrate His Son's birthday by giving people presents and encouraging them to give presents to one another? And if the three Wise Men could come from the East to Bethlehem with presents for His Son when He was first born, why not have a red-faced, round and jolly old man from the North take presents to millions of babies and little boys and little girls and grown-up men and women to remind them how much God loves them? It all made a lot of sense to me, especially after I learned about St. Nicholas, whose name could so obviously be turned into Santa Claus.

Well, after all, I was only a not-too-bright 4-year-old, so none of it was ever difficult for me to believe, any more than it is today. Surely, God doesn't mind our inventing Santa Claus, especially when so many people would feel even emptier than they do, if they couldn't believe in anything. We know that our invention hardly fools anybody over the age of a year and a half in these precocious days, but who knows how many people are moved by a myth to search for the truth? When all's said and done, anything that may help us discover, however many years it takes us, that God did really and truly give us the gift of His baby Son on the first

Christmas Day, at least deserves a bit of pondering — whether in Gimbel's or Macy's or in the person of the kind and generous Salvation Army Santa Claus ringing his bell for the poor on a bitterly cold shopping day around the corner from Christmas.

Ash Wednesday / Lent:
Growing Up Catholic

If a head count means anything, Ash Wednesday is at *least* as popular today as when I was a kid, when, in our house, it ranked with Christmas, Palm Sunday, Holy Thursday (we *always* visited three churches), Good Friday (no truncated versions — three hours, and stop squirming), Easter Sunday, and the Feast of St. Rita of Cascia (my mother was blind for a year and attributed her cure to St. Rita of Cascia, after which she made a novena at St. Rita's Shrine every year, having to take two trolleys and a bus to get there). Ashes cost little, since they are the burnt palms of last Palm Sunday, or virtually every parish in the archdiocese would be bankrupt this week.

We were big on abstinence for Lent when I was a kid. It wasn't difficult because we all liked fish and eggs and a weird soup my mother made that we called simply "brown soup." I grew up to learn that it was made of burnt flour (actually burned brown in a frying pan), water and broad noodles. I can't say that *fasting* during Lent meant a great deal to us, because our regular fare was well within the quantitative limits, except that in Lent we didn't eat between meals and we always went "off" something. With my mother, it was sweets. And with her, there was none of this business of "Sundays don't count as Lent." If my mother didn't get at least 10 souls a day out of Purgatory, there is absolutely no justice whatsoever. Her mouth would water if she knew you were even thinking about a cream puff. I have known some big sacrificers in my day, but when it came to going off sweets, my mother made John the Baptist look like a glutton for eating wild honey with his locusts in the desert.

By my father's edict, we all went off movies, never more than a once-a-week luxury, anyway, both because my father was always suspicious of them and because they cost a fortune — 15 cents (they gave you dishes to take home, obviously recognizing that no movie alone could be worth that much).

The big thing was that we knew Ash Wednesday and Lent were different from any other time of the year. It was part of the rhythm of our lives. We *felt* different during Lent. As I look back, I know that we didn't really go "off" that much, but we did go to daily Mass more often, always Stations of the Cross on Friday afternoon or evening, and confession every Saturday (no point in telling your father you hadn't done anything to go to confession for, after having failed to take the ashes out of the furnace, empty the water from under the ice box and take the garbage out, when you'd been told a thousand times). And you were supposed to be "nicer" to people during Lent.

But it all got you in shape for visiting three different churches on Holy Thursday, with Our Lord in the Blessed Sacrament surrounded by flowers and incense. That was a whole family affair for us, because we always waited for my father to get home from work. Sometimes we met him at the trolley car, which never arrived sooner, no matter how often you left the curb and went out in the street to look for it.

Good Friday was especially solemn for us. Again, it wasn't quite so much what we did as how we *felt*. We felt solemn. We knew that something dreadful had happened some 1,900 years ago, but we didn't feel sad so much as — there's the word again, but I don't know a better one —*solemn*. I guess we didn't feel sad because we knew it had all turned out fine, or there wouldn't have been any Easter Sunday.

Holy Saturday was kind of a day of waiting. Easter was already in the air, and the fact that my mother was counting the hours before she could descend on a cream puff somehow did not really distract her from her deep personal sense of the Resurrection. We always liked Easter. Somehow it was an especially "clean" day, probably pre-cleansed to a considerable degree by the inevitable Holy Saturday confession, which didn't seem quite like the regular Saturday confession, maybe because you had to wait in line longer and by the time you got into the confessional the priest might be cranky, which didn't faze you because it seemed to be part of what Lent was all about.

We were a ham and cabbage Easter Sunday family, with Coleman's hot English Mustard for the ham, and soft-boiled potatoes that were really soft and white. My mother would cook it all and dutifully eat her share before plunging into the dessert she had been sacrificing for 40 days. Her joy was marvelous, and we shared it as a very real part of Easter itself.

I hadn't intended writing about all this — certainly never intended getting nostalgic. But Ash Wednesdays make me that way. I'm glad I was reared the way I was. Nobody ever told us we were being psychologically twisted and spiritually deformed by my mother's and father's old-fashioned ways of observing Lent. Perhaps if they had been more sophisticated I might be more liberated, and not believe a fraction of what I believe today, which is amazingly like what they taught me to believe when I was hardly a half-dozen years old. I suppose I'll always gravitate toward fish on Friday and the Stations of the Cross, and have a Rosary in my pocket. And I will always feel awed by the pope and even by my own auxiliary bishops.

All of which brings me back to the hundreds of thousands who packed our parishes this Ash Wednesday to get their ashes, and who seem to me to be startlingly similar in what they feel to what I felt as a kid. Many of the youngsters could give no more articulate an explanation of Ash Wednesday and Lent than I could at their age. But they *feel* — shall I say "solemn"? And that instant of solemnity when the ashes touched their foreheads will be internalized for a lifetime, as it is for their parents. They may drift away, some of them, but the *feel* will always be there, as it is with their parents. Is that superstitious? Is that what the books warn us about when they tell us of the horrors of growing up Catholic?

Many of the people who pack my daily Lenten morning Masses at St. Patrick's Cathedral, and who watch on television from their hospitals and nursing homes and living rooms, were brought up differently from the way I was brought up, I know. Yet we all seem to be quite comfortable with one another. That's what *faith* does. It transcends the ages, the cultural differences, the modes of teaching and the form of Lenten penances. Even in a day when millions of the diet-conscious reject cream puffs on a daily basis, I'll bet most every Catholic knows what it meant to my mother to go off them and has a *feel* for why she did. Great woman, my mother. Would have shamed John the Baptist into giving up wild honey — and maybe not even eating the locusts on Fridays!

Good Friday:
"Where Were All the Men?"

Pontius Pilate did a lot for me when I was a kid, and I never forget him for it. He was a worse coward than any kid I knew, even myself, and in that he gave me comfort.

There he was, big man in an armor breastplate (I'm talking about the first of the Stations of the Cross as they were in St. Barnabas Church, where my mother and father used to take me on Fridays in Lent because it was closer than St. Clement's, our home parish), and all he could do was wash his hands. He had this huge Roman army, all great big fellows with swords and lances and plumed helmets and white horses, like in "Ben Hur," and yet he was scared to death. Even as a kid, of course, I knew he wasn't afraid of the people screaming at him to have Christ crucified. His soldiers could have slaughtered them. He was afraid he'd lose his job. He was afraid the people would report him to Caesar, that Christ was trying to overthrow Caesar and that he, Pilate would be charged with being soft on an enemy to Caesar.

I had been taught enough by my mother and father to see through the whole thing, but I could still hardly believe that a man who seemed to have everything, like Pilate, could be such a coward. My father told me there were lots of people like Pilate around and that I would come to recognize them when I grew up, but that the important thing was not to be one myself. Naturally, I swore I never would. The whole idea was disgusting to a kid. Sad, what growing up can do to us, isn't it? Another reminder of what Our Lord means in saying, "Unless you become like little children, you cannot enter the kingdom of heaven."

Pilate wasn't the only one who made the Fridays of Lent exciting, however. I used to look forward to the Fourth Station, when Jesus would meet His mother, and the Sixth and the Eighth.

How proud I would be of Mary when the priest would call out the title of the station: "Jesus Meets His Afflicted Mother." It fit right in with the singing of the *Stabat Mater* between stations — sorrowful, haunting, yet so very consoling. I found no difficulty in understanding that Mary was my mother, too, even though my flesh-and-blood mother was standing beside me. And I knew that Mary would do for me exactly what she was doing for Jesus, if I ever got into deep trouble. Just as I knew that my flesh-and-blood mother would.

The Sixth Station meant a lot to me, too. I would do a lot of thinking when the priest said: "Veronica Wipes the Face of Jesus." I would think: "This lady was exactly the opposite of Pontius Pilate. Those soldiers must have given her a hard time, and the people must have laughed at her. But she didn't care what anybody thought. She just wanted to help Jesus. I wonder if I would have done that, or would I have done what Pilate did." As a kid I didn't know the legend of Veronica, except that her name meant "true image," since Jesus was supposed to have left the image of His face on her veil. But that she was possibly the woman who had been hemorrhaging for years until she was cured by touching the hem of Jesus' robe, that I didn't learn until years later.

The Eighth Station always had a similar effect on me: "Jesus

Speaks to the Women of Jerusalem." I knew they were some of the women who used to follow Jesus around, listening to His teaching, and probably helping Him in various ways. But now that He was a "criminal," despised, beaten, about to be crucified, covered with mud and blood and spit — that they would still stand up to be counted as His friends, that really impressed me. And I was equally impressed that Jesus could be so concerned about them, when He was in the condition He was in, telling them not to weep for Him, but for themselves and their children.

Then, of course, very quickly, it always seemed, came the Twelfth Station, and Jesus is actually hanging on the Cross. But who is standing beneath the Cross? Mary and the other women. That, too, awed me every time. It was always the women. I knew about Simon the Cyrenean's helping Jesus carry His Cross, but I also knew the soldiers had forced him to help. So I always came away from the Friday Stations asking myself the same question: "Where were all the men?" The Apostles had run away right off the bat, and not a single man seemed to have come along to take even one of their places. John apparently slipped back at the last minute, and joined Mary at the Cross as the end came, but even he, the "Beloved Disciple," had taken off for his life. But the women stayed, always and only the women.

One thing I learned from it all. No one who grew up on the Stations of the Cross could argue that the Church never appreciated women.

But the one I think of most frequently to this day is weak-kneed Pontius Pilate, who made me feel a lot braver than I really was as a funny-looking little kid who thought he could never be such a coward as Pilate.

Good Friday:
A Cross on Lexington Avenue

It was a miserable day when I first made the Stations of the Cross in Jerusalem, following the route tradition says Jesus took to Calvary. A cold rain chilled my bones as I tramped on the cobblestones. The vendors and hawkers and fishmongers blocked the way with their carts, and my temper flared at their indifference to my pilgrimage.

"Obscene," I said to myself, "going about their business as though nothing had ever happened here."

That's how stupid I can be, that stupid and more. Deep down, although I thought I knew better, I had clearly been expecting kind of a mid-eastern Central Park, with a few romantically winding paths dutifully lined with olive trees. Certainly I had expected it to be quiet and prayerful, to look "sacred," with perhaps (though I would never have admitted this to myself) a discreet strain or two of the *Stabat Mater* accompanying my reverie between each Station.

Worst of all — the rain. Who in the world would ever think it could have been pouring rain on the first Good Friday? I suspect that, more than anything else, the rain changed my entire perspective, even though I was well aware that Christ could still have died on a gorgeous day. It was like a New York rain on a nasty day in an especially dismal March. Not at all a "Singing in the Rain" day. Rather, the kind of day that makes it five times harder than usual to go anywhere — traffic twisted and angry, subway trains and buses packed and suffocating, gridlock building. I can imagine a man trying to drag a cross along Lexington Avenue at 8 in the morning on such a day, especially with a bunch of soldiers pushing and shoving people aside to make room, and being roundly cursed in turn by taxi and truck drivers — "Why don't you do that at night, instead of in the middle of the rush hour?"

Somehow the events of the first Good Friday suddenly became even more horrifying to me when the thought struck me that people could have been actually going about the business of living while Christ was engaged in the business of dying. To think that His trip from Pilate's palace to Calvary, far from being the most tumultuous event the people had ever witnessed, could have been for the majority of them nothing more than a *nuisance*

— this did something to me that the best theology and Scripture teachers (through no fault of their own, my classmates know) never got through my extraordinarily thick head.

I know. I know the Gospel says a great crowd followed Him en route to Golgotha. I know the impression St. Luke creates, that huge multitudes of people were screaming up at Him on the Cross — people who had presumably been part of the whole parade. I'm not arguing with that, at all.

It was only that as I, myself, slipped and almost fell on the cobblestones that day in Jerusalem, as I noted personally for the first time that the street is sharply graded, uphill and down, as I in real life pushed my way through the vendors, between the narrow walks — I suppose, to be honest, that as I felt *myself* ignored, the sheer loneliness of Christ hit me as never before. What word am I looking for to describe what it feels like to be trivialized? I suppose the number of people doesn't matter, if you have a sense that most of them don't care.

Some did, like the legendary Veronica, said to have moved in on Him and dried His face. I guess the rain and the cobblestones made me recognize that she might well have been one of several nuns I know in the South Bronx, wiping the faces of the poor. Or a Jewish lady whose shop I pass on the way to work. She's a nice lady who always smiles at me, and I can imagine her hustling out of her shop with an expensive towel or a silk scarf, to do precisely what Veronica did. I suppose it's outrageous to think that today Simon the Cyrenean, who, according to St. Luke, "was coming in from the fields" on the first Good Friday, might be a bag man huddled in a doorway or lying on a grate. What odd thoughts I come up with. But surely the "Daughters of Jerusalem" who wept at the sight of the broken Christ would be our archdiocesan Ladies of Charity, so utterly anonymous in their goodness.

I felt quite alone, at first, on that day in Jerusalem, and quite annoyed, at first, at the business-doers who seemed to pay as little attention to me as to the path I was trying to follow. But before it all ended, they had taught me a lot. They were doing precisely what they should have been doing, without the slightest intention of irreverence or contempt for the fact that maybe once a Man had possibly dragged a cross somewhere near the current cobblestoned street on which they live and move and have their being — or maybe on a similar street long buried a hundred feet beneath the current one. They taught me a lot about translating the sentimental. They reminded me to "see His blood upon the rose . . . His face in every flower . . . His cross in every tree" — *today*, not merely 1,900 years ago.

And I remember even as I write, that at least one of the vendors was selling roasted chestnuts, just as on Fifth Avenue. That made even the cold rain smell sweet.

Easter:
All Brand New and Shiny

A new suit every four years, because you'd grown hopelessly out of the old one, was worth the wait, particularly since it usually meant new shoes, for the same reason. Sixty-eighth and Buist was not Fifth Avenue. It wasn't even New York. But it was "where the guys hung out" in Southwest Philadelphia, in their new Easter suits, some costing as much as $12.50. It was our Easter Parade, and never mind how cold the wind when Easter came early, or how thin the suit (even then, cashmere didn't come at $9.95), there you stood, shiny and new and maybe shivering.

A new tie was always a nice touch for the stationary parade. You could keep looking down at it, admiring its blues or browns or purples or reds. Color coordination wasn't a big thing at 68th and Buist, only cost (imitation silk could run as much as a quarter) and *newness*.

After all these years, Easter to me is still that same sense of *newness*.

Small wonder that the first reading of the Easter Vigil is from the first chapter of Genesis, the book of creation, the story of the beginning, when God looked at everything He had just made and "found it very good."

Small wonder, either, that for centuries every imaginable symbol of newness has marked our Easter celebrations. The very sunrise is filled with special meaning. The night is gone — not merely a night like any other that has ended with daybreak but "nightness" itself seems gone forever.

What is the Easter Bunny except the refraction of the miracle called spring, teeming with new life?

I don't know why no one ever made the connection for us kids in new suits, our sisters in new dresses, our mothers in new hats (even Irving Berlin could never convince my mother that a hat was a bonnet) — the connection with the early Christians. The newly baptized all wore white gowns during Easter week. Those previously baptized wore new clothes. Both symbolized, of course, that they had risen to new life in Christ. So the whole new-clothes thing at Easter was really a profession of faith in the Resurrection of Christ.

Customs do change, even Catholic customs. The eggs and fish we substitute for meat today during Fridays of Lent were not always seen as such. In fact, eggs were once forbidden during Lent, so that giving them as gifts on Easter Sunday, especially painted with bright new colors, was another sign that a new day was born after the darkness of Lent. The Middle Ages being what they were, it didn't take much for the Easter egg to symbolize the rock that was rolled back from the tomb of Christ, and the Easter egg roll was born!

All such efforts to express the wonder of newness, however, pale in comparison with the renewal of our baptismal vows during the sacred liturgy of Easter. As we have gone into the waters of death with Christ, the waters symbolic of His tomb, so we rise with Him in our new life of baptism. As we renew our baptismal vows, we plead for and commit ourselves once again to the new life of innocence that came with baptism itself. That's a wonderful moment in the new Easter liturgy, perhaps one of the most wonderful to accompany the renewal we call Vatican II.

But through all the years, right up through this very Holy Week, I have never experienced the sense of newness more elatedly than after a good confession. Whatever was is all gone. However minor or major the sin, it's washed away. I'm sure that started when I was a kid, not infrequently scared to death of going to confession, but the result today is precisely the same — the wonderful feeling of being all shined up and polished and ready to take on the future, whatever it might bring. Today we wisely call it the Sacrament of Reconciliation, for so it is, but it's still the Sacrament of Penance, as well, and I'm happy to do whatever I'm supposed to do to be given the absolution that means complete purification, total newness once again. Which reminds me that I went to confession in Rome recently, and was, for the first time in my life, given the Stations of the Cross as a penance! I swear it had to be my poor Italian. He couldn't *possibly* have understood me! But it's a good reminder.

I won't be wearing anything new this Easter — many things old and a few things borrowed, like Cardinal Cooke's cassock, and a clean shirt with clean socks (always a must for me when I offer Mass on such a day), but I'll *feel* new and will be deeply grateful to the Risen Christ that so many others will feel new, as well.

And all the while, as I catch glimpses of the Easter Parade on Fifth Avenue, I know I'll be thinking of the corner of 68th and Buist, where the guys may possibly still hang out — and of a kid shivering in the wind on the corner with his thin ($9.95) but shiny new suit, and marvel that God has brought him to New York for these Alleluia years of his life.

Easter:
His Special Cross

He couldn't get out of bed for any one of the final Easter Sundays of his life. About the only thing new we could give this one-time snappy dresser was a new set of pajamas. The priest would bring him our Risen Lord in Holy Communion, and if I were anywhere in the United States I would get to see him before the day ended.

My father *felt* all dressed up on Easter Sunday, however, even when he could feel little else. It was for him without a doubt the day unlike any other day of the year, particularly since most of the other days were Good Fridays, even Christmas. That's the way it is with a proud man who becomes helpless. To have the Bon Secours Sisters shave him and scrub him, bathe him and dress him and change the sheets beneath him when my mother could no longer do any of those things — that's not what a man who always walked tall envisions for the final five years of his life. But Easter Sunday made sense in 10,000 ways, often without a word.

Perhaps that's why I was saddened a bit by the letter to the editor of *Catholic New York* telling the world that I shouldn't say such foolish things to lepers as, "God reserves His choicest sufferings for His closest friends." I felt bad, I guess, because it was my father who taught me that. I don't believe that for a single moment during those five final years — or in the years when his illness was "coming upon him," as we always put it — I don't believe he ever thought he wasn't one of God's close friends. And that without a shred of vanity.

I would have died rather than deprive my father of his belief that by joining his sufferings with those of Christ he could help save the world, in some mysterious way that he never insisted on understanding. I can't imagine his looking at me with anything but pity if I told him God wasn't responsible for the suffering in the world. He knew that far better than I did, because he knew God far better than I did — hence, he knew more *real* theology than I have ever learned. He would have told me: "That's not the point. I *know* God doesn't bring suffering into the world. I *know* human beings do this, whether as individuals or nations, but since the world is full of suffering, I'm highly privileged that God lets me share it with His Son in a very special way, and use it for others."

Big on justice was my father in his prime, but were he alive

today he would have been horrified to have his cerebral arteriosclerosis blamed on anybody else. Nor would he have wanted
anyone "credited" with it. It was his special cross and my mother's,
for whom it got heavier every day, as she took two trolley cars and
a bus to visit him. It was as much part of her life as it was of his,
and both of them understood it as a gift of God.

I wish I could just once in my life preach an Easter Sunday
sermon even half as meaningful as the one my father preached
each year, just by lying there in his new pajamas, so clearly *feeling*
it was Easter.

All Souls' Day:
Loyalties That Do Not End

It's too long since I've visited our family plot in Holy Cross
Cemetery on the edge of Philadelphia, but I could walk to it
blindfolded. That's because of the many Sunday afternoons my
father walked me there during the years that he was growing me
up to understand that family loyalties don't end with a funeral.

I liked the walk. I liked being alone with my father, and I
liked especially our regular stop at Alessi's, after leaving the
cemetery. Mr. Alessi sold tombstones from the front yard of his
house and the house always had the fresh smell of newly cut stone
— and of extraordinarily robust red wine, made by Mr. Alessi's
own hand. I couldn't have been more than a dozen years old, but
my father never objected when Mr. Alessi poured each of us a
water tumbler full of the dry red richness that only many years
later would I learn was Chianti. The walk home, a good three
miles, was always both bracing and mellow, and always very
nostalgic.

I had only the vaguest recollections of my father's mother
and father, or of my brother, Joseph, who had died when I was a
child, but I would always feel very close to them when we would
kneel on the ground beside the little headstone, which was all that

distinguished our lot from hundreds of others. Not that there
weren't some big, shiny, handsome headstones, with names cut
into them deeply and proudly by an Italian stonecutter who could
have readily competed with Eric Gill, or magnificent tombs that
would have done King Tutankhamen proud. But most families
like ours had simple plots, level with the ground, so the grass
could be cut more readily — and cut it was because my father had
paid for "perpetual care."

Our ritual would always be the same: first the Our Fathers
and Hail Marys on our knees, rain or shine, or however wet and
cold or frozen the ground. Then an inspection of the limestone
with the names of Thomas and Mary O'Connor and Joseph
O'Connor, their grandson, my brother. Next came the head shaking and I knew my father was wondering anew what had happened to the years and how he had become an orphan as a grown
man. I learned to shake my head, too, stirred by some dim
consciousness of the fragility of life, and that one day I would be
walking my own son to this hallowed spot to teach him to pray
with me for the father who then stood beside me holding my hand,
and for my mother, who I knew must one day die as well.

In my fancy, it would be the same walk from the same house
in which I was being reared, for I never dreamed of ever leaving
it. I always felt a little pain in my chest, then, in thinking of a future
without my mother and father, but the pain was never for them,
because even as a little boy I knew they were good and would go
to heaven. That's the way I had been taught, so I could never think
of death as a loss for them, but only for me.

My father died on an October afternoon when the leaves
were falling. I never knew anyone who appreciated color more
than he. In his working years he would mix his own paints, never
buying any ready made. He would crush the pigments and he
would tell me about cobalt, the beautiful blue I came to love, and
I know my pride was forgiven when, just a few years ago in the
ceramic center of Italy, Faenza, I amazed a ceramic artist by
remarking that there must be a lot of cobalt in the ground there,

because such haunting blues dominated the ceramics. I was right, and I knew my father was smiling. It was fitting that the cemetery was brilliant with reds and yellows and purples on the day of his funeral, and especially golds. He was a master goldleafer.

It was on a November morning just two years later that we reopened the grave. Thanksgiving had ended and the colors were subdued now. That was fitting for my mother, with her subdued temperament. She never tried to compete with anyone. As the years pass, my awareness of her person deepens. I think of John W. Lynch's long poem about Mary, *A Woman Wrapped in Silence*. I have come to recognize that my mother was a woman of quiet dignity, exceptional dignity. There were pools of quiet deep within her, pools from which I have spent much of my life drawing strength.

I don't worry much any more about not having shown my love adequately for my mother and father when they were alive. If they didn't know then, they surely know now, as I do.

It's too long since I visited the family plot that still has one grave free. Once I was ordained and it was clear I would never have a wife or children of my own, the whole family assumed that grave would be mine, the grave of a single man. Instead, I will be buried with my spiritual brothers, in the midst of my spiritual family, beneath the high altar of the great Cathedral of St. Patrick, whenever God so determines. But in the meanwhile, my loyalties remain what my father taught me they should be, loyalties that do not end with funerals. I shall never lie in the grave of my forebears, but I will visit them soon, now that the leaves once more cover the earth. All Souls Day might be a wonderful time, or thereabouts. After all, it's only an hour and a half, or so, by train to Philadelphia, and a trolley ride of 20 minutes would take me as far as Alessi's. Maybe his son still makes that wonderful Chianti.

Mother's Day:
"My Mother? Who Is My Mother?"

There is no way to make the words sound warm, cozy, or sentimental. They had told Jesus His mother was waiting for Him. "Who is my mother?" He said. "Those who do the will of my Father in heaven, they are my mother . . ."

But were the words an insult to Mary? How could they have been? They defined her perfectly and with the highest accolades in Christ's unlimited vocabulary. They defined her as she had defined herself when invited to become His mother: "Behold the servant of the Lord."

I would like to be able to write a Mother's Day essay that would fill the eyes of every mother in the world with tears of joy and pride. I could, indeed, write endlessly of my own mother's love for me and of the love I have seen pouring from the hearts of countless mothers I have known for the countless children they have borne. I can get quite as mushy over precisely the right Hallmark card as anybody I know, and how often I searched through the years to find exactly the one that described my mother.

But when I dry the tears of nostalgia, what is it I remember best about my mother, and what did she do for me that was infinitely more important than anything else she could have done after bearing and feeding me? I remember most my mother's always asking herself, in her own very simple way, whether it was "right" to do this or that, whatever the "this" or "that" was. It was her way of trying to determine God's Will. She wasn't a theologian; she was a mother. She seemed to be quite clear in her mind that to be a mother, she had to try to do what she believed to be God's Will.

I sincerely believe that this was far-and-away the most important thing she ever did for me — really to take seriously that very early question in the old "penny" catechism: "Why did God make me?" And its answer: "God made me to know Him, to love

Him, to serve Him in this life, and to be happy forever with Him in Paradise." I have forgotten it ten thousand times. I have failed to live it a hundred thousand times. But my mother never seemed to forget it and never failed to live it. And because of that, I at least always know when I have forgotten or failed — a priceless gift in itself.

I'm not sure how my mother would have reacted had she been waiting for me outside a house, only to be told I had asked, "My mother? Who is my mother?" I can only guess she would have left in a huff. She wasn't Mary; never pretended to be; would have felt it sacrilegious to be thought of as such. And the Lord knows she never thought of me as Christ! But I'm certain she would have understood: "Those who do the will of my Father in heaven, they are my mother . . ." That would have seemed very natural to her.

Leave me out of the equation altogether. Leave my mother out. Just ask for a moment what Mother's Day might mean if every mother asked if her own motherhood could be defined as Jesus defined motherhood, and then decided that, whatever the past, that was to be the goal of her own motherhood: to do the Will of God on a daily basis, in every thought, word and action. What would be the impact on the children of our land? What would be the effect on society at large? Imagine television's defining motherhood as Jesus defined it. Imagine the newspapers, the magazines, the tabloids, the radio, the talk shows — all assessing, examining, reporting, rewarding the accomplishments, the contributions of mothers all over the land in terms of their doing the Will of God as they perceive it.

Utterly absurd, I know, as so much of what I write and preach. Absurd as Mary herself, whose heart was pierced with a sword, so that many would come to know her Son.

Every Mother's Day I think of the way my mother died, early in the morning, sitting in my sister's home, praying the Rosary. I can't imagine her dying not praying the Rosary. Nor can I imagine her not praying the Rosary that her kids, myself among them, would always remember their catechism, about knowing and loving and serving God.

Thanksgiving:
Immensely Thankful for a Gift

"What a neat way to die," said the 5-year-old daughter of my friend, Peggy, when she learned of my mother's death. And it was. My mother died precisely as she lived, quietly and unobtrusively and praying her Rosary.

She almost made it for another Thanksgiving. I had called her only the day before to tell her I would be home for Thanksgiving. That always made her happy, for there had been so very many years when I was far away. She was at my sister's when I called, and that's where we would have our Thanksgiving dinner.

I was having breakfast on a Navy ship in Norfolk when a call came in for my host. He excused himself, came back in a moment and told me the call was for me, and I knew. While there hadn't been the slightest warning — my mother at 84 seemed impregnable — I knew she had died before I picked up the phone to hear my dearest friend compassionately telling me so, and suffering in the telling.

We had our Thanksgiving dinner together, my sister and her family, and buried my mother on Saturday. That would have been her way.

But it's how it came about that was "neat." My mother was an unmercifully early riser, and when she stayed at my sister's, she would put the coffee pot on for the family long before anyone else had stirred. She would then go into a little den off the dining room, sit in her favorite armchair and pray her Rosary. Sooner or later my sister or her husband would appear, and take two cups of coffee back to their bedroom.

It was my sister's turn this time. She went for the coffee, detoured to wish my mother a good morning, and found her at the

fourth decade. It was a Tuesday, so she would have been somewhere in the fourth of the Sorrowful Mysteries — Jesus carrying
His Cross. She was to complete that particular Rosary in heaven,
"where sorrow will be no more, nor mourning, for the former
things have passed away."

I am shocked to recall how many Thanksgivings ago that
was. We were very close, my mother and I. It's frequently the way
in a family with a priest in it, no matter how many other kids there
may be. I wager that 9 out of 10 priests in ordinary circumstances
head for home on Thanksgiving Day, especially if their mother is
alive. My problem was that for so many years of my life I was in
extraordinary circumstances. At sea, overseas, maybe someplace
in a hole in the ground, where one tends to romanticize Thanksgiving more than a little, and to hear Bing Crosby singing 10,000
miles away that "the folks are the friendlier, the roads are the
dustier, the pies are the crustier, way back home." That's a less
than accurate rendering, I know, but the years are many.

The sun seems colder these fall days, without the leaves on
the trees to warm and color it. I would be untrue to my father's
uncommon sense if I rebuffed the reminder of my own mortality.
It's all around me as the grass itself grows gray. I know I will be
wondering this Thanksgiving Day how many more such days
there will be. I'm grateful to a mother and father who made such
wondering the most natural thing in the world. It makes me feel
neither sad nor old to think such thoughts. Not sad, because I was
taught from earliest childhood that I was created for an infinitely
greater world than this. Not old, because I was taught, as well, that
death is a second spring.

I will be immensely thankful on Thanksgiving Day wherever I may be, thankful for a million billion things, but above all
for the tremendous gift of faith, which prepares me as nothing else
for whatever happens on any day of the year. It makes for a neat
way to die.